This is a book about hands: hands that break us, hands that heal us. And so we are touched as we open to both the grief and vitality of Cynthia's story and, within it, the compelling stories that were triggered and eased by her healing hands.
— Deena Metzger, *Writing for Your Life*

Bodies Unbound is about the journey of a woman who found something to love in everyone she worked on and ended up loving herself. It is a journey of healing, inspirational and uplifting.
— Diane Zuckerman, *Daily Camera*

Cynthia gave voice to her own experience and gave sacred meaning inherent in a life.
— Susan Crane, *Denver Post columnist*

This will appeal to individuals committed to personal growth who have sympathy for the human condition. Cynthia gives us a startlingly honest account of her life and short vignettes from the lives of some of her clients. It is a fascinating story, one I read straight through without pause. It's powerful and poignant, but a wild ride, and not a book for the faint of heart. Waring tells her story boldly, unself-consciously, apparently unashamed of the messiness of life. She allows herself to be healed on many levels, and she becomes a powerful model and servant to her clients. Bodies Unbound is full of inspiration and warmth.
— Mary Vineyard, *Massage Magazine*

I picked up Bodies Unbound in the afternoon. Except for a bathroom break, I didn't put it down until I had finished it, late at night. As I read Cynthia's story I laughed, cried, shook my head in acknowledgment, shook it again in amazement, felt judgmental and then forgiving, questioned the "ethics" of giving such accounts, then realized I had been reminded of my own shadow issues. Finally I felt deep gratitude for having been privileged to share a spiritual journey along a holy, though rock-strewn path. It is extremely well-written and totally engaging, this book is destined to be a best seller, not only to massage professionals, but to all who are seeking the path to inner healing, forgiveness and love.
— Jack Thomas, *Touch Therapy Times*

Here is a modern woman's journey through the underworld of alcohol, drugs, loss and despair. With deep insight and psychological honesty Waring peels away the layers of a wounded heart to reveal a resilient and tenacious soul on a long but rewarding healing mission.
— Ron Liggett, *Boulder Books*

A must read for those committed to emotional and physical healing. "Bodies Unbound" is an unusually powerful book.
— Gillian McIntosh, *Whole Life Times*

We store life experiences in our bodies. Waring masterfully illustrates this by sharing her own story and that of her clients, thus motivating us to become aware of our own bodies. I highly recommend this book...
— Laurie Grant, *Reiki Master and Author, Enlightened by Angels and Unlimited Reiki Manuals*

Cynthia Waring is a dangerous woman. she has lived life to extremes. Becoming a massage therapist, and the self-discovery that followed, changed all of that. Her difficult journey through loss, incest, alcohol and drug addiction, near constant moving—50 times in 10 years, because the "intense pain, confusion and chaos was home to me"—is chronicled in her book Bodies Unbound: Transforming Lives Through Touch. This book details the most harrowing moments of her life, when a carefully constructed self finally hit the wall of truth, leaving no way to go but through. Every page of this book sings with courage, honesty and forgiveness.

— Janine Gastineau, *WordPlay*

Bodies Unbound

Transforming Lives Through Touch

Cynthia Waring Matthews

To my son, Russell, who said, "It stops with us."

Acknowledgments

I would like to thank my mentor, Deena Metzger, who led me, by example, to speak my truth. Thanks to my beloved husband, Wyn Matthews, who taught me that it was safe to love again and patiently assisted me in editing this edition. Special thanks also, to my fellow students in Deena's classes who encouraged and listened to my stories as they were discovered and first formed into words. I also wish to thank my dear friends, Linda Powers, Odette Springer, Kevin Bellows, Raina Paris and Jeanette Dyer, who supported me through this arduous journey and lent me their courage and inspiration when I had none. I am grateful to those who helped me edit this book in its various forms, especially Judith Huntera, Jacqueline Darrigrand and Sharon Weil, whose wisdom, love and generosity have supported and nurtured me. I am thankful to Christopher and Pausha Foley who never lost their belief that my book needs to be available, and for their many hours of help in sending Bodies Unbound into the world again. Finally, my gratitude goes to all those brave men and women who openly and unguardedly told me their stories, letting me know I was not alone.

Contents

Acknowledgments   4

Introduction   8

A Voice   16

Signs   24

The River, the Fire and My Son   28

My First Massage   40

Getting Started   43

Smoke   51

Mrs. Adams   55

Hoover   59

Sam and Babe   62

Massage of the Heart   67

Stories   71

Katherine   72

Stewart   76

Jan, Muktananda & Kirpal Singh   78

Lola   84

Stars   88

The Countess   91

The Lamb   94

The Shadow Side   98

Memories Emerging   107

Creating a Cocoon   111

Breakdown   115

Sarah   118

Katrina   120

The Tear   122

Mimi   124

Unraveling the Mystery   127

Old Main   132

The Queen   135

The Concert   142

Epilogue:
The Cry of the Ancestors   145
The Author   153

There were two pictures on my bedroom walls while I was growing up. Lying in bed to my left was a Hummel print. An angel held the hand of a little girl. The angel pointed up to heavenly realms. The little girl looked down at a small snake. To my right was an autographed picture of Cousin Fred, famous for his group called "Fred Waring and the Pennsylvanians" and for inventing the blender. He was a vision, in our family, for all the success in the world.

Introduction

I LOVE BODIES. I love every shape they come in. I love their smells, their texture, and their heat. And I love touching them. I have been a masseuse for thirty-three years. The veins in my hands are like rivers. When I lay my hands on a body, just put them down on warm, soft flesh, I am in ecstasy. I love intimacy. I love knowing secrets. I love to get to the core of things. Every time my work takes a person deep into the center of her being and she remembers the beginning place of contraction and how she protected herself out of fear, I feel fulfilled.

My parents wanted me to be a pianist. I wanted to be a singer and sing with my Cousin Fred. He was famous for his musical group, Fred Waring and the Pennsylvanians, and for inventing the blender. Luckily for me I became a masseuse and learned the art of intimacy; of being in the body. I had the hardest time being in my body. I experienced passions and fears I couldn't control. My body was haunted so I lived in my head. Now when I catch myself "thinking" instead of "being" I take my attention and I put it in my feet. I feel the sensations in my feet. When my feet are tingling with attention I take the effervescent feeling into the tissues of my calves, the miracle of the knees, the magnificence of the thighs into my favorite place—the pelvis.

Many of us, especially women, have been talked out of being in our pelvises. I believe it started a long time ago when men decided to become fathers. Before this their role in a woman's life was that of lover or son. When they decided to become fathers they had to control women's sexuality so they would know who their children were. To do this they created religions making sex a sin and horrible punishments for women enjoying their bodies. They created chastity belts! Thousands of women are sexually mutilated each year to this day. Its called female circumcision. I believe it's time we made friends with our pelvis and brought sacredness back into sex.

When my pelvis is alive with sensation I bring the energy into my belly. This is where we digest our experience; assimilate the outside world. Then I bring the energy into my lungs and heart. My heart has a broken-hearted feeling. The world tends to break our hearts. Some say it's how we learn compassion. When I'm in my heart I can't imagine hurting anyone. When my heart is open and I'm in love with all humanity I bring the energy up into my vulnerable throat and my fragile face. I feel the areas around my eyes and mouth. When I am alive with sensation from head to toe I focus on my thoughts. I free my mind of negative thinking;; all those plots and plans, ideals and dogma. When it is free of all thought I know I am ready for infinite possibilities. This is what I mean by being in the body. This is what I mean by Bodies Unbound — that experience of being alive and embodied in the present moment.

I became a masseuse through a series of accidents in 1976, within months of leaving a convent. I went into the convent to avoid the pain of my life, to rise above it by escaping into spirit. But God knows the difference between love of Him and fear of pain and my days in the convent were numbered. I believe God knew the way to my heart was through learning the sacredness of ordinary life and the wisdom of the flesh, and I learned this by becoming a masseuse.

I have always enjoyed watching bodies tell their stories. I have spent hours at cafes just watching. There are so many lonely, sad bodies, drooped over, pelvises tilted, hidden under layers of tension. Necks that have lost their curve, flat feet, compressed chests. And then there are the runners, demanding their endorphins for the day like Catholics, their tongues hanging out at the rail, beat horses, hyped on their own adrenaline.

And there are bodies that walk like sticks; heads on top of tight necks, shoulders stiff with pride, stomachs touching backbones. They do not eat. They are not nourished.

Some bodies sway and swish as if walking to the beat of Caribbean music. They melt into chairs, into doorways. They flow past parked cars like a vision.

And sometimes I see a body that bounces along, free as a let-go balloon, fresh as new leaves in spring, and I wonder, how can anybody be so joyous? How did she escape the crippling effects of our civilization? Where is her shame, her mask? What kind of person made that kind of body? What is her life like? What is her story? Through massage I have found my answers.

I have given more than thirty thousand massages in the past thirty-three years, arriving with table, sheets, and oil at the homes of strangers. I've massaged every type of person, from movie stars to babies; old women dying of cancer—no breasts; men from war—no legs. I've been a masseuse to young girls as a present from their mothers like some initiation rite. I've been a present to lovers on birthdays, coming to their house with balloons tied to my bag.

I've massaged in hospitals, country clubs, beauty shops, exercise salons, hotels, out by swimming pools getting sunstroke and in bedrooms getting scared. I've had jets sent for me by the rich and people calling for all kinds of sexual perversion.

I've massaged women who have just been raped, mothers who have lost their children. A soap opera queen cried every time I touched her; she couldn't tell me why. People have remembered every kind of emotional and physical abuse on my table—which made me remember mine.

My clients have shown me the parts of themselves they never showed anyone before. During massage, they have been open and vulnerable with me, and it was in this state of being that I was nurtured as well. My clients' trust in me allowed me to see myself as valuable. Through their eyes I saw my strengths, my courage, and my ability to love. I listened to the woes of my clients like a confessor and told them stories of my own. They let me in to see their bruises from facelifts, asked for my prayers when they couldn't get off drugs, called at 3:00 a.m. when they'd been hurt by bosses, lovers, or friends. I would go to them to help them make friends with life again.

All the ways in which a person feels shame, bewilderment and other thoughts usually kept private were common topics on my table. My clients begged me to get rid of their fat. I'd listen to the pain and grief hidden in that flesh, first with my hands then to their cries as the sorrow worked its way out of their bodies in the form of tears and memories. I was told about sexual problems, affairs, and hilarious, almost unbelievable stories.

I listened to my clients' nightmares and massaged their mothers when they came to visit. My clients would say, "Knock some consciousness into my mother, would you?" These mothers had usually never dreamed of having a massage. They were women who had never heard about "positive thinking" or "affirmation" or "reflexology." They had never heard the words "emotional abandonment" or that it was all right to grieve. Many of these mothers had never had anyone on their side before. They were shy when I said they had nice legs or hair. They cried when I touched their faces gently. They'd tell me, "Please don't tell my daughter I feel unappreciated," and I never did. These were mothers I never saw again.

Sometimes family members would give their father a massage. It was always a surprise for his birthday. The family thought Dad would love this gift, but most of the time he didn't. I could tell he felt vulnerable and was terrified he might become aroused. My touch created anxiety rather than pleasure. It was as if I was torturing him. And when I massaged other males of our species—brothers, sons, uncles, friends—my hands on their bodies stirred up every kind of sexual dilemma possible both in them and me.

My clients never invited me to their parties or sent me postcards on their travels. In public my clients would hide. They hid from me in grocery stores, their carts filled with puddings, cream, and whiskey. I would turn my head not to embarrass them. I didn't care what they put in their mouths. I just wanted them to love themselves. I wanted them to be able to say in the mirror and to all their friends, "I ate every bite, and what's more, I loved it."

The life of a masseuse was not always pleasant, deep and touching. Many people sneered when I said I did massage. I could tell they thought, "Whore" or "Servant." Clients would call at the last minute and be outraged if I couldn't come. Sometimes I'd drive half an hour to get to a client, and then he wouldn't be there. I had no insurance and little respect. Wealthy people often quibbled about five dollars

The following were common phrases I came to expect: "Is your oil natural?" "Don't ever touch my stomach." "I want it upstairs— can't you carry your table upstairs?" "Don't get oil in my hair." "I hate it when you rock me." "Harder." "Lighter." "Massage me while I'm on the phone." "I have to catch the news." "I still have that knot!" "Can't you come later; I want to go to bed after my massage?" "If I'm not here, just wait." "Don't mind the dog." "Change the music." "Take a message." But no matter how difficult a person was I usually found the loving part of her, or perhaps I should say, massage found the loving part.

Being a massage therapist changed me as much as it changed the people I worked on. At first I discovered my immense need to be needed and to please others at all costs. Both men and women brought every kind of temptation to my life, and I fell into one pit after another. It took a long time before I could say, "No, I will not come to your house at 4:00 a.m." "No, I will not wait for you for two hours without getting paid." "No, I will not lug my table up two flights of stairs," in the home of a weightlifter. "No, I will not massage you when you are drunk or stoned."

Finding the confidence and self-love to say, "No" to those demands was like going to the bottom of the ocean to dive for pearls. And how I found them, those words, those pearls, now there's a story.

I am also dyslexic. Dyslexia is a visual/brain dysfunction. It is difficult for me to interpret what I see. My understanding comes from touch, emotion, and spoken words, not letters on a printed page. Because of this I couldn't plan my life in the ordinary way. So my life just happened. I couldn't read the newspaper to find out what was going on, so I had to depend on information coming to me from an unseen source. Perhaps this explains my profound interest in spiritual matters. I even discovered my dyslexia by accident when I was thirty-six years old, eight years after I began doing massage.

I met a man at a lecture who was an ophthalmologist. I had a reoccurring eye infection that had been going on for nine years and caused me great discomfort. He noticed it and asked me to come to his office to find out the cause. It turned out he had written his thesis on dyslexia, and was passionate about it. Before I knew it, I was hooked up to graphs that monitored eye movement such as how often I reread a line or how many times I fixated on a word. He gave me a 100-word story to read. When I'd finished reading, he asked me ten questions about what I'd read, and I couldn't answer one of them. I will never forget the panic I felt when he asked me a question and I didn't know the answer. It was the way I had felt in school, which had led me to think I was stupid. I remember the way the roots of my hair hurt from embarrassment and shame. I could read the words. I recognized them. But the meaning of the words wouldn't come to me, and I never knew why. I discovered through the tests that I have no short-term memory. I have to do things slowly, without anxiety, in several different ways in order to learn.

By the time I slowed down enough to understand what I had read, we discovered I was reading below first-grade ability. The ophthalmologist had a program that trained the eyes and mind to work together more efficiently. I participated in it for six months, and those classes changed my life.

I remember after the training finding a radio schedule in a newspaper. There was a blues program a few days later. I love the blues. I remember writing down the time, the channel, and the date of the program. I even located the program on the radio dial. When all those details came together and I began listening to the blues on the appointed day, I couldn't stop crying. I suddenly became aware of my isolation. I had been living as though on a deserted island in the middle of the ocean, having to wait and accept those things that drifted up on my shore.

Because my mind could not fathom information from the printed page, the choices of events I could attend were limited to information that came to me from conversations. I now had insight into problems that had embarrassed me all my life. So that was why I always said, "Left" when I meant, "Right." Or why I was always going "down" to San Francisco and "up" to Mexico." That was why I never knew about stories on the news, magazine articles, or famous people whom everyone knew about. When I told my son, he said, "So that's why you can't play Pac Man!"

After the training to remedy this disorder, I learned how to use the banks, which I had never understood. They were too complex. I liked to hand people money and have them hand it to me. It was a nuisance paying bills with cash, however, and a friend convinced me of the efficiency of checks. I had always used the pockets of my coats in the closet as my bank. When I fished out all the money from the pockets and counted it to take to the bank, I had ten thousand dollars. I had no idea I had so much. It had been collecting there for years. My clients would hand me money, and I would bring it home and put it in my coat pockets. When I needed money, I went to my closet.

Soon after that I began to write and, for the first time, discovered what I thought. My life had been about feelings and touch.

It has been an awakening for me to discover the words to describe the moods and stories of my life, the clients I have known and loved, the men I have known and lost the tale of my beloved son, the child I adore. But finding these words has been a slow process. This book is the result of that effort. It has grown slowly, like bone and muscle.

Being focused on the present, and so connected to my clients, I have collected their stories through my hands. When I write about my clients, their memory fills me so completely that they seem to be right next to me. Their stories are clamoring inside me, crying out to be born.

1

A Voice

IN APRIL OF 1983 a friend was in Los Angeles for the summer while writing for a TV series. We both suffered from insomnia. We made a pact that if the monsters in our heads were more than we could bear we would call each other. We only let the phone ring twice. If the other person was up we called back. If by some miracle we were sleeping, two rings wouldn't seriously wake us up.

On one of those sleepless nights Gary and I were on the phone. It was spring. I was in the kitchen. While talking, I cleaned. I swept the floor, cleaned the top of the stove, washed dishes and wiped any grease spots off the walls without missing a word. I could recite a recipe by heart to someone on the phone while hanging a picture on the wall. It is something I picked up from my mother. It is nervousness while in the home that can only be soothed by industry. It is a way of declaring, "I am here. I am worthy."

Gary talked on and on about his problems with the TV show, the plot, the people involved and the actors. I listened until my kitchen sparkled. In a lull I asked, "Gary, how did you become a writer?" He was off and running until dawn. Had my phone cord been longer or cordless phones been invented I could have cleaned the whole house.

He said, "I lived in New York City in a seventh floor apartment in SoHo. I decided to kill myself. In order to do this I crawled across the kitchen table to get to the window to jump out. On the table was a pad of paper and a pen. I decided before jumping that I would write a letter explaining my suicide. Dawn came, I was still writing and I thought, "I won't leap from the window, I'll become a writer."

With those words, "I'll become a writer," my entire spine began to vibrate. I leaned against the wall to keep from falling. I knew at that moment that I would be a writer too. My body told me. I imagined my angels and guides filling my kitchen, nudging each other with their wings.

A few hours later a client came to my house for massage. When she was on my table, lying there with all the confidence of youth and beauty she asked politely, "What's new?" I told her, "I've decided to become a writer."

Instead of laughing she said, "Oh, you want to be a writer, you have to take Deena Metzger's writing class. Here's her number."

That day I called Deena who said I could start classes with her in the fall after her summer break.

I was getting divorced from my second husband. My son was visiting for the summer. That weekend was Memorial Day. I made the seven and a half-hour drive to our family cabin in the mountains. Mom was there and delighted we came. I was lit up by my revelation about being a writer. I don't believe I cried once over my soon to be ex-husband. I was in a state of grace. Illuminated by the possibility of being a writer, I ignored the high seas I was heading for by getting divorced.

The "high" didn't last long. It was a long painful summer and my anxiety about my new life alone created feelings that should have been medicated. My emotions rushed over each other like panic-stricken people looking for an exit from a building on fire. While I hugged my son, took him to the beach and went shopping for his favorite foods my insides were in turmoil.

Staring at the vegetables in the market I couldn't decide whether to buy tomatoes or corn. "Red. Yellow/green. No, red. Cucumbers." Hysterically I'd run to the phone and call a friend.

Gary and I met in Cafe Casino most mornings while Russell was at swimming practice. Gary encouraged me to write. I hung on every word as I sipped my coffee. He was fascinated by my life as a masseuse. I was surprised. I told him about the intimacy of massage and he drooled. I told him about hoisting Mrs. Adams on the table with her flesh hanging off the bone and Mrs. Vander who had lost both breasts to cancer and he was envious. He said he'd never been that close to anyone. I tried to massage Gary once. He hated being touched. Everything tickled or hurt him.

One morning, alone on my $60 sofa, filled with obsession, every atom in pain, I made a cup of coffee, ate a piece of chocolate cake, took out my pen for the very first time and began to write. Spiders spun their webs in the corners of the room, ice took over the freezer and moths multiplied in the dry good cupboards to their hearts content.

Writing didn't calm me but it told me things about myself I hadn't known before and I was fascinated. Before writing I hadn't the faintest idea what I thought. I was stuck in "pre-verbal" stage development. My first writing is embarrassing. It is filled with clichés. It is the worst writing I have ever read. I have saved it.

I began writing things I hadn't planned to write. It was as if the words came streaming out of my pen without thought. They were filled with insight and information I needed. Through writing I realized I always hooked up with a man and lived my life through him. My men acted out my dreams and I, not knowing there was any good or worthy thing within me, took care of them.

Beneath this awareness came the knowledge that all my attempts at love would never be fulfilled until I was true to my own needs. I saw a tiny speck of fire within me. It was small and delicate and easy to miss. I dedicated myself that day to the protection and needs of my flame.

This in no way stopped my pain, but I touched something in me that was my own. Looking at these words now, 20 years later, they are more profound to me than ever, even though the image is trite. This was not about being the daughter of a concert pianist or the relative of Fred Waring and the Pennsylvanians. It was a longing to discover what I, Cynthia, was capable of. It was the moment I became obsessed with my Self.

Tom moved out on August 15th, 1983. I remember lying in bed and listening to the sounds of his leaving for the last time. I remember the garage door opening, his car backing out and driving down the alley, the sound of his car growing fainter. I felt fear, emptiness and loss swirling inside me, felt the ache of all his roots entangled with mine ripping away, but I never wanted him back. Even though I almost died from loneliness, insecurity and fear, I never wanted him back. Even if I could have looked into the future at the next, lonely, insane, Plutonian eighteen years I would not take him back. Tom drove away and we were never friends. We never spoke the way some couples do. We have rarely spoken since that day he left. When all sounds of his car were gone I leapt from bed and opened his closet and each drawer of his dresser to stare at the emptiness. My heart was a drum. But, I did not want him back.

A few days later Russell left for the winter to live with his father on the East Coast. The next day, September 3rd, I went to my first class with Deena. Just getting there was a task. Deena lived up Topanga Canyon on top of a hill at the end of many turns. The road decreased in size and quality with each turn-off . The last road, a dirt road, pitted and gouged with ruts, was suitable only for jeeps in bad weather. Deena's house was at the end of this dirt road, which she shared with her three quarters wolf, and sole companion, named Timber.

I had a bad cold. I was in shock because of the changes in my life. There were eleven others there, none of them friendly. I don't remember a word Deena spoke that night, but I remember feeling as though I were beginning my life.

When she finished speaking she gave an assignment. We wrote about a place that moved us. We were not to mention ourselves, the writer, in any way. I described a place in the mountains by my family cabin. Here it is:

It's evening on top of a mountain. On the mountain is a very special tree. There are granite steps, three, that lead to the tree. They are flanked on both sides by large, unclimable stones. The air is so soft, without a breeze or a cricket. There are no shadows as the sun is off this spot of earth and illumines only the high peaks in the near distance. Pinecones and needles cover the ground under the tree and in a ten-degree radius beyond its branches. The dark green needles are in contrast with the golden carpet. A ground squirrel runs up the trunk and off to bed."

I began shaking when I learned we had to read what we wrote. My mouth went dry. As I croaked out the words I'd written my paper rattled. When I finished reading Deena said, "It's very important to tell the truth. When you say the squirrel went up the tree, don't say he went to bed. There are no beds in pine trees. Next."

I was humiliated.

That night driving home, down the twisty road of Topanga Canyon to the Pacific Coast Highway, I sobbed. After I read my pathetic little piece Deena asked me to introduce myself. I said I had a vision I was to be a writer. The room filled with awkward silence. Deena wrote later in her book, Writing For Your Life, "there was no evidence that Cynthia had a chance of ever becoming a writer." To declare at that stage that I would be a writer, in that group, was like stating to a Catholic that I would be Christ.

I felt hostility and was embarrassed at my presumption. This was not a 12 Step Meeting where every timid step towards a goal is applauded. Writing class was a proving ground where the truth of your sight was tested by the words you chose. The only way to know if you had achieved your goal was seeing tears stream down the cheeks of your listener.

For some reason, connecting with my soul's purpose gave me the strength to endure this humiliation. I wanted to be a writer more than I cared about being embarrassed. Though my personal writing was dark, I found in class that I could only write things with a happy ending. I wrote cute things. Funny things. I didn't want to hurt anyone with ugliness

In class Deena said, "One needs to learn to write about the world objectively but from a position of one's own truth. Don't make up anything. See what's there."

She did not know what she was asking.

One evening, about six months into the class, during a break I asked Deena, "How will I ever get into my depth?"

Deena was thrilled. She said, "I've been waiting for you to ask this question."

She told me she wanted me to write about why I had gone into the Order. I had mentioned this as a way of telling Deena I had done something unique. I had tried to impress her. The next few weeks that was my assignment. I wrote that I went into the Order to know God, to become spiritual, to offer others a safe haven, to find peace, etc. Each time I read this she would say, "That's not it."

After a few weeks of this I was as curious as everyone in the class as to why I had joined the Order. Everyone was rooting for me. A bond had developed between the members of the class and I'd become comfortable there.

Brad, a member of the class asked, "What was it like in the Order? What did you do? What time did you get up? Maybe if you try to get into the specifics of being there you will know."

That was the guidance I needed. That night, driving home, I remembered the first day in the Order. I remembered drinking the beer to get the nerve to approach that ominous house. I remembered how I felt abandoning my son and breaking the heart of my mother. I remembered craving cigarettes; sneaking down the stairs to the basement to smoke in the middle of the night. I remembered detoxing from alcohol and drugs. I wrote it all down at home and brought it in the next week.

When I'd finished reading there was complete silence in the room. I was afraid to look up. It was the first time I had allowed the members of the class to see me so clearly. I hadn't gone into the Order to help others but because I was so in need myself.

Deena was thrilled. She found this much more exciting and interesting than any ideal. It also rang of truth. She said, "You got it." And I had. It was the first time I entered and wrote from the depth of my own experience. Everyone in class was moved by my openness. I learned it was a sacred act to open the heart of others through your own vulnerability. I drove home that night with my heart pounding with pride and wonder at my success.

Soon after, Deena took us on a guided meditation in which we were to find our muse. It was a wonderful rainy, lightening filled night. Perfect for a meditation to find a guide from another plain. We were led through fields and tunnels, over walls and finally to a cave where, on the left, was a door. When I entered the room, to my amazement, I found a theater. All the seats were empty. I knew it was my job to fill them. My dogs came bounding down the isle to lead me up to the stage. As I stood there looking at all the empty seats I thought, "Do I have to fill this theater all by myself? How am I ever going to find something to do that will attract this many people?" No voice answered. I was merely met with the resounding certainty of it.

My dogs led me back stage and out through a door where I found myself on a path. Down the path came an old man with a bald head and shabby clothes. I asked him who he was. In answer he changed costumes and laughed as if to say, "Do you recognize me now? How about this way? Like this?" Finally I became aware that it was Shakespeare. I stood there with my mouth open. William Shakespeare was my guide.

I asked him why he had come to me and he said, "You have been to the depths of human experience and I have come to show you the humor of it and help you master words." I made a date with Shakespeare the next day to meet my typewriter.

It was soon after this I began to write about being a massage therapist. A client remembered a traumatic event from her childhood while I gave her a massage. This event had been buried in her flesh for 35 years. Her story affected me deeply. I wrote it down and brought it in to class. No one spoke for minutes after I read it.

They were stunned. I had found my voice. I had found my subject. I had found my life.

I offer it to you with all my heart.

2

Signs

IF SOMEONE HAD ASKED ME what I wanted to be, I never would have thought of being a masseuse. I simply needed a job. It was hot. My feet hurt.

I was walking through a seedy, little shopping mall, looking for work. Grass grew through the cracks in the sidewalk. I'd applied at a health food co-op, a place they sold exotic fish and a hardware store when I saw a sign in a health spa window. The sign read, "Masseuse Wanted." I thought, "I bet I could do that," and I went inside and applied for the job. The manager was a sophisticated French woman and she had just received roses from her fiancé. I always thought it was because of this that she never asked if I'd been to massage school, if I had a license, or even if I'd given massage before. I hadn't. She said I would have to come back the next day to massage the owner.

Going home on the bus, I saw another sign. It read, "MASSAGE" in great big letters. I got out at the next corner and walked back to the massage office. I planned to ask someone there to show me how to give a massage. I was just about to ask the masseur on duty when it occurred to me that he might take a dim view of someone right off the street asking him to teach her his profession. Standing there, needing to say SOMETHING, I asked him how much he charged. When he told me a massage was $35, I said, "I'm sorry, but I don't have enough money." Plus I was not prepared to take my clothes off in front of this stranger, no matter what the cost. I was turning to go when, to my surprise, he said he wasn't busy and he'd give me one for free. Not knowing how to say, "No" to this offer, I suspiciously took a shower as he instructed. With great trepidation, I lay down on his table. While I was lying there waiting for him to come into the room, I realized I could memorize what he did. Then I would know how to massage the owner of the health spa the next day. Very pleased with this chain of events, I could hardly wait for my massage to begin.

Not only had I never given a massage before I'd never had one either. In fact, I'd just gotten out of a convent. The sisters there didn't believe in touching. Prior to that I had spent years and years at spiritual pursuits practicing techniques to numb and suppress my body. I had stared at blank walls following my breath for hours. I had chanted myself into a stupor. I had prayed on my knees on hard wooden floors, eating nothing but brown rice and miso soup, hoping to purge myself of all my demons. It had been so long since I'd been touched that I felt as if I'd never been touched before.

When the masseur came in he turned on a tape player. Music from heaven filled the room. He began the massage with my feet. I heard angels singing. He opened the dammed-up rivers in my thighs and calves. I sighed, letting go of tension. My arms came alive in his hands. I felt blessed when he touched my face. My back was restored as waves and waves of feeling surged out my arms, down my legs, up into my face, into my belly, around my head, and splashed over the boulders in my back. Finally I knew that I had found what I'd always been looking for. I had always been looking for a kind, gentle place where I could feel at home.

I was in awe. I didn't know the body could feel such pleasure without feeling guilt. Not only were my knots being broken up, but emotional armor was crumbling too. I felt whole, ecstatic, integrated, loved, and calm, all at the same time. After all my searching for a god from all the gurus, in all the ashrams, churches, religious orders and drugs, I had never felt so holy as I did on that man's table. I felt accepted and cared for, even loved.

I, like everyone else I knew at the time, believed the body could lead me astray with its feelings and desires. I had tried to stifle my body, to make it feel what it was "supposed" to feel, not honor how it truly felt. I don't know how many times I'd heard, "You shouldn't feel like that," or "You should feel grateful" or "ashamed" or anything but what I was truly feeling.

I had fought against this training, but the punishments our society puts on a girl enjoying her body are immense. I had suffered tremendous guilt for my sexual desire. When my mother learned I had discovered sexual pleasure via masturbation, she gave me a book written by a doctor that said if a girl masturbated she would go insane and never be able to have a relationship with a man. Mom and that book scared me to death.

A life of passion, of following the body, the physical manifestation of the soul, I have found, is a difficult life. I didn't follow the rules. Consequently, I didn't know anyone with similar life experiences. Often my life was such a mess that I didn't know where to turn or how. Then, as if my own experiences weren't hard enough to bear, there was every form of judgment against such a life. There is Christian religion with all its taboos, rules of being I'm sure Jesus never intended, then Indian philosophy saying, "All manifestations are an illusion; rise above everything you can see, taste, touch and smell." These ideas perpetuate the message that thought, or even nonexistence, is a higher form of being and that somehow we are supposed to ignore our bodies.

On the masseur's table I had the experience of pure being. My body and spirit weren't separate. I felt like a priestess, an ancient one who could lead her people into rites of passage and rituals uniting them with the wisdom of the body.

At last I knew what I wanted to do with my life. I wanted to anoint all my brothers and sisters with oil. I wanted to bring their minds and souls and breaths of life back into their bodies, their earth. I wanted to witness their sighs when they came home. I wanted to roll away their blocks of shame, to break up their knots of guilt and despair, to unite them with their senses and passion—their nature—to make them one with the honor and wisdom of that nature. I knew I wanted to be a masseuse when I left the office of that wonderful man whose name I never knew. I didn't want to fix the body I wanted to comfort the body. I guess I needed to "mother".

I went out on the street and waited for the next bus feeling confident. I had an experience of well being. I had found a place for me and a purpose.

3

The River, the Fire and My Son

I HAD LOST ALL CONFIDENCE in my own feelings, in my ability to know what to do, when I saw the sign "MASSEUSE WANTED." I didn't know what I thought. I had lost everything that was dear to me. I had walked away from what I loved the most, my son, Russell.

Phil was my first husband and Russell's father. Phil and I met in 1966 at San Jose State. We could not have been more different. Phil had started the underground newspaper there and was at the hub of student politics. I barely knew Reagan was governor. The noises in my own head screamed louder than anything outside myself.

Phil brought me a new world that seemed to matter. He brought me the world of Vietnam. He brought me Africa, civil rights, Birmingham, injustices from around the globe, and the plight of people who looked like I felt. I was so overwhelmed with gratitude for finding some form of life that was meaningful, something real and visceral, something important, that I couldn't separate this feeling from the source, Phil. I admired him tremendously. It took me a long time to see that "political" people tend to love others abstractly; they don't love their smell or stare deeply into their eyes or embrace their weaknesses.

Oh, and how my parents hated Phil. He was a "communist," a hippie. He had a beard and wore sandals with socks and Bermuda shorts. His hair went beyond his ears, he wore John Lennon glasses, and he was against the war in Vietnam. And Phil, with his brilliant, Jewish, photographic memory, knew every law the U.S. government was breaking to go to war. And he brought all this up at dinner in front of my parents' Protestant, Republican, wave-the-flag ideals. My parents could not have been more horrified if Phil had been black and deformed.

I became pregnant after being with Phil four months. He said he wanted to marry me, so we moved in together right there on campus. My parents disowned me, and I got caught up in the excitement of it all. The night before our wedding I admitted to some girlfriends that I really didn't want to get married. I was scared. I didn't think I loved Phil. They made me call Phil and tell him. We cried all night.

The next morning I kept the appointment I'd made at the beauty parlor, and there, under the dryer, I began to miscarry. Phil was called, and he took me to a hospital. There they gave me drugs to prevent the miscarriage and sent me home. Friends came over to see me. They brought the school newspaper, which ran the story about Phil and me getting married in the school chapel, and that the president of the school was coming. How could I get out of the wedding? It was right there in the paper.

With the drugs, my miscarriage slowed down. I called my history teacher and asked him to walk me down the aisle. Phil's best man was wanted by the police for blowing up a building along with some other SDS members, so we had a lookout posted for the Feds, another one for my father, who had threatened to stop the wedding; and another for an old boyfriend of mine who had just arrived home from basic training and was threatening to abduct me. Phil's mother, Sylvia, was crying her eyes out and refusing to speak to anyone because Phil wouldn't let her walk him down the aisle in the old Jewish tradition. I was having contractions and was stoned on codeine.

After the reception Phil and I drove to Carmel for our honeymoon. On the way I began bleeding heavily, and we ended up at a hospital, where I had a D&C. The baby was lost, but there I was —married.

Being married to Phil was an adventure. A few months after the D&C we went to Europe and hitchhiked from Madrid to Istanbul.

When we got back we settled in Cambridge, Massachusetts, where Phil went to Harvard and I got a job to pay the rent.

The marriage looked idyllic and it made a good story, but I was unhappy. I did not know how to love. Being close to someone terrified me, and in marriage there is no escape. I ended up coping with my terror by misusing drugs and alcohol, which had been my friends since high school. Then I got pregnant again. I didn't want to be pregnant. I didn't want to be married. I looked in the paper every day at the "For Rent" section, planning and dreaming of a life of independence from responsibilities, of romance and adventure. I didn't want to be a secretary. It didn't matter that I worked in William James Hall, where I met Erik Erikson and Professor Jerome Kagan. I felt stupid around all those intellectuals.

I was not in love with Phil until the night our son was born, when Phil rubbed my back during contractions and hid himself in the food cart outside the delivery room so he could be close to me in case I needed him. My heart cracked open with the birth of my son, and then I loved his father.

I gave birth to my son, Russell, named after Bertrand Russell, on November 3, 1968, at 8:05 A.M. in the Cambridge City Hospital after a long labor. I loved him from the moment I saw him.

While he was still a baby, I would wake him from a sound sleep just to hold him. I could stare at him for hours, just watching him breathe. I thought up songs for every occasion: songs for waking up, songs for going to sleep, songs for putting on shoes and socks, and songs for taking a bath. I nursed him for his first eight months. I became obsessed with health food. I couldn't stand the thought of anything remotely resembling a chemical entering his or my body.

I could not keep this up, however. After a year of trying to be the perfect mother, I became restless and harried. I broke my kneecap ice-skating and had to manage my fourteen-month-old son alone while in a cast from ankle to thigh. It was winter and I couldn't go out for fear of slipping on the ice. I felt that Phil and I lived separate lives, in two rooms close to Harvard College. Phil was on campus, either studying or leading rallies against the war. He didn't know I said good-bye each morning with a smile induced by speed, greeted him each evening in an alcoholic stupor, and got to sleep by smoking hashish. Sometimes I wondered what they taught there at Harvard. I felt so alone and so scared. I was terrified I wouldn't do the right thing for my son, terrified I couldn't resist the pleasures that kept attracting me.

Oh, the things that took me away from my baby, the things that deprived me of being a mother. The lure of the perfect high from acid, gurus, or miracles. My old college roommate, Judy, now a flight attendant, flew in once a week to Boston with the best drugs the 1960s ever made. It was the year of Woodstock, the year America marched on Washington, and I was home washing diapers after countless shots of Ouzo and myriad tokes of grass, waiting for a husband who was out doing exactly what he wanted to do.

I tried to be a good mother, but it seemed the only way to be a mother at all was by taking enough drugs to keep away the anxiety. Ultimately, drugs scrambled the messages from my subconscious that would have warned me of an impending disaster.

One day while my old college roommate was visiting, we took acid together and hitchhiked out of town for the day, leaving my son with a baby-sitter. At dusk we realized how late it had gotten, and I was desperate to get back home. The acid was wearing off . Reality was setting in. I began to re-enter a world where being responsible was important. I began to notice the broken beer bottles in the park, the used condoms, the oil spills in the parking lot. We saw a couple kissing in a nearby car, and we asked them if they could take us back to the city. And he said, "Why not?"

Had we looked at them closely, with clarity, we would never have got in the car. The man in the driver's seat was huge, well over three hundred pounds. When he smiled, I noticed his teeth were discolored and rotting. When the woman turned around to greet us, we noticed her eyes weren't on the same plane in her face. She looked like a Picasso. She had her long black hair in a tight ponytail. Her lipstick was smeared all over her face from kissing.

When we were arranged in the backseat and the doors were firmly closed, the driver screeched out of the park like someone mad and haunted. As we barreled down back roads, over hills, and around curves, just missing parked cars by inches, Judy and I held on for dear life. Our eyes were as large as golf balls. The man never slowed down as we neared the city, still off the main streets. We entered a one-way street going the wrong way. A sign that clearly said, "DO NOT ENTER, KEEP OUT" didn't faze him a bit or slow him down. We crashed through the sign, drove on the sidewalk and in the road, where there were huge holes in the pavement made by bulldozers. We crashed through sawhorses supporting warning signs, throwing them everywhere. We drove across lawns and over curbs and finally onto a main street right in the center of Cambridge, where we screeched to a halt at Harvard Square. "This okay?" the driver asked. Picasso turned around and smiled sweetly, exposing her toothless gums. Much later I realized the ride represented the life I was leading. Picasso and her old man were creatures lurking in my psyche, driving me to create one crazy experience after another. They were the parts of me I did not know, who stole from me every form of beauty and blocked out every bit of grace.

But at the time I didn't know about the shadow side and my drinking got worse, further impairing my judgment. Three incidents convinced me to leave my son. In the first incident we were playing on a beach. Russell wanted to go into the ocean in a yellow rubber boat some friends of ours had brought. I put Russell in the boat and pushed him out through the waves. I was swimming alongside, pushing him farther and farther out, when a huge wave came and crashed over us. When I came to the surface and looked around I could not see the boat or my child. I began diving into the murky water, panic flooding my body. I was hysterical, diving and coming up for air. I kept thinking, "He's underwater and I can't find him.

How long can he make it without air?" Someone finally swam out to tell me Russell was on the beach. His naturally buoyant, two-year-old body had been deposited on the shore by the wave. I shook for days. It was as if my body was trying to shake me into some awareness.

Several days later the second incident happened. While driving home from the ocean, I ran a stop sign and was broadsided by a car that had the right-of-way. I didn't run the stop sign deliberately; I just didn't see it or the car or know I was driving at all. Russell and I were not hurt, but I became terrified, and Phil was beside himself.

The last event took place at a wedding for some friends of mine. I got very drunk, then asked for some speed so I could stay awake to drive home. I remember putting Russell in his car seat and backing out of the driveway. That was the last thing I remembered for the next two hours. I came to my senses just in time to recognize the turnoff to our street. I had driven two hours in a complete blackout with my little son in the car. When I became conscious, Russell was staring at me. I didn't know if he was trying to speak to me or trying to reach in and find his mommy. I don't know why he stared at me. I can only imagine and remember the times I stared at my parents, bewildered, wondering, "Are you there? Is anyone home? Am I here or am I invisible?"

Phil and I were divorced in 1970. He wanted custody of Russell and I agreed. I really didn't know what that meant. I didn't know how my life had been defined and protected by the needs of my son and my husband. Russell was almost three; I was twenty-four. I was so young that I didn't know the decision to leave Russell would cause me so much pain. I didn't know the human heart could suffer so much without dying. Perhaps it was this need for a family, this need to mother, that drew me to massage therapy.

When I left my son and his father, I walked and cried and drank for months. I had no home. I was on the streets living in abandoned buildings with people who had also abandoned all hope or struggle. I felt as if I was on an endless walk in the desert discovering the deceit and falsity behind every illusion. I reached a state of hopeless degradation and despair and wore out every possibility of escape.

I finally realized that I'd made a terrible mistake. At the time I left Phil and Russell, I knew leaving would be hard, but it was much harder. It was worse than I could have imagined as I crawled out of my despair and my flesh awakened from the shock of misuse. I jolted out of the numbness that I was experiencing when the realization that I had truly left my son set in.

Each morning I awoke thinking I was still with my son and husband. I could hear the sounds my son made, the cooing as he woke from a nap or a night's sleep. "Mommy, Mommy," he would say like a cat purring, like a brook murmuring.

When I realized the truth of where I was, on an uncovered mattress in an abandoned building where I ate food from cans, I would feel a stab in my heart. When I knew that I was dreaming, that my son was not really there, the pain spread from my heart down my arms, filled my stomach, and raced down my spine. "He is not here," the pain told me. "Your son is not here. You left him."

And the emptiness over the loss of my son would not be filled. I caved in around that black, empty space. It pulled me in headfirst.

The numbness began to wear off one day while I was drinking tea in a health food restaurant in Harvard Square, where I made salads and washed dishes. It was a tea made from reeds found in the desert. As I put the cup to my lips, I knew that neither the tea nor anything in this world could touch or comfort me. I had left something behind that I could not release. I became a shrine to the loss of my son.

Phoning old friends did not help. Rushing into the arms of men did not help. Smoking grass did not help. Nothing helped. My son's bewildered face would rise before me, float above me like a moon I could not reach. He came through the haze of every binge. There was no thought or dream he did not enter. It was as if he were the dream, the sleep, the mist, the hole, the star, the moon, the grief, the abyss, the nightmare, the dinner, the prayer, the God, the beating of my heart, the razor, the wrist, the blood, the blight, the fog, the rain, the mud, the sun, the pain, the silence, the torment.

I drank the tea and silently screamed and drank the tea and silently screamed. The tea made from reeds found in the desert— long, thin, green reeds that separated into sections so easily, not like my son and me, no, not like us.

Oh, yes, I was free now, free to get raped while hitchhiking, free to cry myself to sleep every night thinking of my son. I was free to drink myself into a stupor, free to take enough drugs to become an addict, and free to wake up with major anxiety attacks. I was free to do all of these things over and over and over again, until some blessed inspiration burst forth in my brain.

The man I was living with had an affair with a friend of ours who came to visit for the weekend and wouldn't leave. I thought to myself, "I won't kill myself. I'll join a convent."

Choosing a convent was not an out-of-the-blue decision. I had been prone to mystical experiences my whole life. I had been involved with yoga, Sufi dancing, Indian gurus, Christian mysticism, palmists, astrologers, I Ching, runes, tarot, sweat lodges and rituals of all kinds. I hoped the convent would help me escape the mess I'd made of my life and give me direction. I was grateful to find a place where I could rest and recover.

This tendency to go off the spiritual deep end looking for a savior was balanced by my obsession with sex. I would swing back and forth between sex and spiritualism, experiencing a broad variety of possible lifestyles. I would be a saint for a time. Then I would hit a certain degree of safety or boredom and toss all my hard work into the air. I would break the spiritual part of the cycle by doing something so outrageous that it would take several months for my own psyche to comprehend what had happened, let alone friends and family. This would lead to feelings of degradation, which would eventually lead me to pious acts of penance.

After I had been in the convent a week, I began to detoxify from a gallon of wine and a pack of cigarettes a day and all the drugs I had been on for years. I never told the sisters why I was so sick. I think they thought all the evil of the world was coming out of my mouth, my bowels and my pores. It's as good an explanation as any, I suppose.

After a year I became restless again, and I knew I had to leave. In the Celtic religion my name, Cynthia, is the name of the Goddess of the Moon, and like the moon, I am always changing. The phases of the moon are present in me. I do not control which side faces where or how much of me faces the sun. I was forty-five years old before I learned to have faith in those moments of darkness and change, to simply endure.

The day I left the convent I was cooking lunch for the twenty women living there. I was also high from drinking sherry, which I should have been using to marinate the roast. A beautiful man came to the back door selling fish. He asked, "What are you doing here?" I answered, "I don't know."

Within minutes I had packed my tiny bag of belongings and was riding down the road next to him in his beat-up old pickup truck, which reeked of halibut. There was a song on the radio by a group named Hot Chocolate. Ricardo sang to me at the top of his lungs, glancing at me seductively while driving at breakneck speed into the fading light of day. He sang, "I believe in miracles since you came along, you sexy thing."

I had been aware for two months that I would not be able to stay in the convent much longer. The realization came to me when I read a letter from my mother about my son visiting her. She had found him in her bedroom while he held up my picture and kissed it through the glass. I could imagine his seven-year-old hands holding the only thing he could find of me. I was sure there was not a trace of me to be found in his own house. The only thing his father and stepmother allowed him were my letters and my down sleeping bag, which I had left him when I went into the convent. Russell and I called this sleeping bag "The Blue Cloud." He said he liked to sleep in it, but he didn't use it often because his stepmother made him stuff it back in the bag each morning all by himself and that was very hard to do.

I could not remove these images from my mind: my son kissing my picture and stuffing The Blue Cloud along with all his feelings of mother back into a small bag in the morning. These images yelled at me, "Wake up, wake up." So when the fisherman came to the back door of the convent, I knew he was my ferryman.

I moved back home with my mother and stepfather in their walnut orchard in the San Joaquin valley, where I had been raised. I sat in front of the fireplace on cold, foggy December nights and watched the prunings from the walnut trees burn and turn to ash. I stared at the fire for hours, feeling at home with the flames. My parents stared at me, then at each other, afraid of the emptiness I had become.

There was a dirt road that went beside our walnut orchard and through fifty acres of asparagus behind the trees. This road led to a river, where I sat on a footbridge made of rope to watch the water. I walked there each morning at dawn through fog that came all the way down to the ground. I felt wrapped in a shroud by the damp softness and surrounded by something ethereal, impermanent, ghost like. Sometimes, as I walked down the road, I played a bamboo flute my mother had made as a young girl. One morning Don, who owned the asparagus field, was checking his levees when I came down the road playing the flute. I nearly scared him to death. When he finally saw me, I could tell he was badly shaken. He said he kept hearing this eerie sound, but all he could see was the fog. He thought he was losing his mind.

When I went home to the trees of my childhood, I realized what an alien creature I had become. Living in strange places, I couldn't tell who I'd turned into. I had to go back home and measure myself. The things I used to walk under now hit me in the chest. All the houses looked smaller, the long dirt road looked shorter, the faces of the neighbors were more wise or more shallow.

My son came to visit me that Christmas. I hadn't seen him for a year because I had been in the convent. At the airport we were both struck by the force of our emotions. Neither of us spoke. Thank goodness there were people around us to make some noise and help us remember words like "hello" and questions like "How was your trip?" I had held him in my heart day after day, trying to bring back the way he looked, to make some connection with a picture I took out of a secret place; now the real person was too much for my mind to comprehend. I was overwhelmed with fear at the sight of my son, and I could tell he was terrified of me.

I did not feel safe with Russell until he had closed those gigantic brown eyes and was sound asleep in the soft warm bed of my childhood. I could stare at him by candlelight and once again watch him breathe. I sat beside him like I sat beside the fire and the river, just watching him. While I was sitting there something began to stir in me. Something began to touch me. It was the need Russell had for me that called me out of my lethargy. The fire and water could engage me, but they did not need me.

The way my son loved me, and the way he patted my face felt primal, connected to the earth. There was something warm that reached to the core of me and let me know there was no one else in the world who could take my place for him. This knowledge came as a shock and a blessing. It gave me someone to be; a mother.

Ten days later, when I borrowed Mother's car to take Russell back to the airport in San Francisco, I thought I would die from grief. I watched him walk onto the plane, his eyes full of tears. Panic flushed his face and my heart as I watched the feelings he couldn't hide capture him and hold him prisoner. I could do nothing. I could not hold onto the one I loved; his father had custody of him. I couldn't save him or myself from these feelings; I could only watch. The world felt like one large prison.

We came together and separated, came together and separated, for eight more years, growing together and ripping apart. It was a slow, tortuous growth.

After I left him at the airport, I drove to Sausalito and walked the streets trying to connect with what I saw and felt. There I met two men, and the three of us spent the evening dancing. I remember very little about them except that they were not from the United States, and they were kind. I danced first with one, then the other. Their arms held me together until I grew new skin and my bones hardened. I danced with these men until there was enough of me back in my body to safely drive home.

When I got home, I realized I could not stay in my mother's house or in that community any longer. A few days later I packed my things and moved to Los Angeles.

I moved with two goals in mind: to create a life that supported freedom, and to make a pleasant, safe home in which my son could come to visit me.

So when I saw the sign that said "MASSEUSE WANTED" and something inside me said, "I can do that," it wasn't out of arrogance or an unshakable belief in myself. It was more like a miracle. Life had opened herself up and said, "Here, we found a place just for you."

4

My First Massage

WHENEVER I REMEMBER going back to massage the owner of the health spa I wonder, "How did I do it?" I walked into the office and met the owner, who led me to a back room, where she took off all her clothes right in front of me. She handed me a bottle of oil and lay down on the table, covering herself up with a towel.

Before, when I'd set up this appointment I'd thought, "There's nothing to it. Rub a little oil into someone's skin, move your hands in various ways and pronounce them massaged." Now I viewed massage as a holy ritual.

Standing there before the owner of the health spa, the one who expected me to touch her expertly at any moment, I froze. I went completely and totally blank. I couldn't remember a thing the masseur had done on me the day before. Fear raced through my arms, legs and heart. Then I heard a voice in my head give instructions. They were not "Build an ark" or "Change this water into wine." They were "Do something. Pour oil in your hands. Put your hands on her foot and start rubbing."

I was aware of my heart thumping as I poured oil onto the palm of my cold hand. It took every ounce of courage I had to put my cold, shaking hands on her foot.

I realized an amazing fact as soon as I touched her. When I put pressure on her body with my hands, they stopped shaking. The warmth of her body warmed my hands.

I was glad she had her eyes closed. I had poured far too much oil in my hands and had to wipe the excess off on my arms. And, with one hand on her foot, massaging all the while, I leaned over and put more of the extra oil on my legs. I felt like an acrobat in a circus. As I worked my way up her leg, I wondered how far it was proper to go. What if I touched something I shouldn't? The towel was in the way. I couldn't see where I was going. What did I do with the towel? Any minute now I was sure she was going to open her eyes and say, "This is the worst massage I've ever gotten. You haven't the faintest idea what you're doing."

Sweat poured off me in the hot room; maybe I would faint. I kept looking at the clock, wondering how long to give each part. Ten minutes had passed, and I was only up to her knee. How did I get from her hip to her stomach? Did I take the towel down from the top, uncovering her breasts to do her stomach, or lift it up from the bottom, exposing her pelvis? Either way embarrassed me. Did I do both legs first or go around her in a circle? Did I massage her arms while she lay on her back or while she lay on her front?

As I neared her head, forty-five minutes later, the idea of touching her face made me cold. I don't believe I had ever contemplated the intimacy of a face. Not only that, she hadn't said a word. She just lay there. I didn't know if she liked what I was doing or not. Was she even alive? What was she thinking?

When I asked her to turn over, my voice shook. I waited a full minute to get the nerve to speak. Had I done enough on her front? Was I enough? All I knew for sure was that she was oily. I wondered what she'd do if I left. I could just walk out the door. She would never know where to find me.

When the owner of the spa turned over, I found I was more relaxed with her on her stomach. Her face was down. She couldn't open her eyes and catch me staring in confusion at her body, wondering what to touch next.

There was no way I was going to finish the massage in an hour. With ten minutes left, I had half a back, an arm, and two legs to go. I said, "I'm running late." She said, "Take your time."

Her voice was dreamy, like she was enjoying it—like she never wanted me to stop. A trickle of confidence seeped into my veins.

Take my time? What a concept. They'd never said that when I was a secretary.

And with the confidence that followed, I remembered the way I had felt the day before when the masseur had massaged me. I concentrated on my touch. It was my voice. I was singing to her hips, opening them to freedom, unlocking the doors, stretching, soothing, and caressing. It was my song, like a brook babbling; swishing through the rocks, over, under, around and down. I swished through the curve of her back and into the knots in her neck and over her buttocks and down her legs; going slowly, backing up, faster, then ebbing and stopping at a place, holding, pressing, then letting go—and my song was over.

I don't know if they needed a masseuse so badly they would have hired anyone with two hands who said, "Yes" or whether she truly liked my massage. Whatever the reason she said I would do, and that's how I became a masseuse.

5

Getting Started

MOST OF THE WOMEN who came to the spa where I had my first job were elderly. I wandered around in a white uniform trying to look helpful. I gave them a hand getting out of Jacuzzis, stinking of chlorine, and found them extra towels. When someone wanted a massage, I was paged over a loud speaker.

Almost everyone I rubbed had suggestions: their last masseuse had put the towel just so, heated their oil and cracked their neck. My massage was "simple," they would say.

But what I lacked in knowledge about strokes and anatomy I made up for in sympathy. I could listen to and understand anything. My misspent youth was finally coming in handy. I understood their hangovers, headaches, bad marriages, their desire for a new religion, their need for my prayers, their desire to lose weight or gain weight, their worries about their children. I would listen like some confessor and tell them stories of my own that would inspire another story from them, and on and on we would go until we knew each other like old friends.

While working at the spa, I never felt as though I took a mind or soul to a deep realization of their inner truth. I was too shy, too unsure of myself, too nervous. It was later that I realized I couldn't take anyone more deeply into their lives than I had gone with myself.

After I had been a masseuse for three months, I decided to get some training. I wanted to learn a routine, to know the names of the bones and the muscles. Not knowing the names of the body brought up old fears of not knowing things I was expected to know. When the fear grew intolerable, I called three massage schools, picked the cheapest one, and two days later became a student.

This was not an expensive New Age massage school where they taught every style of massage. Nor was it a school that played music of birds chirping by a waterfall or raindrops and wave music. I went where they trained women working in massage parlors. I didn't know that when I signed up, but it became obvious very soon.

The massage parlor ladies, most of whom were Asian, were tiny people with long black hair and soft, bell-like voices who chattered like brooks. Their gaiety impressed me; their lives shocked me. They survived by catering to men's lust, men who were dying to be touched, who only wanted sexual pleasures. The instructor would show them a Swedish routine, but the moment his back was turned, I would see them in the corner walking on each other's backs, light as leaves, balancing along the spine, laughing and talking a mile a minute. I'll never forget one woman coming out with, "I keep saying, 'No hunka punka, no hunka punka,' but he no listen." All the other women in the class laughed as she pantomimed his prick under the sheet.

I was curious about the massage parlor ladies but never wanted to be one. I was going to be a healer, a savior. Everything nice, safe and respectable. No hunka punka on my table. I would give the word "massage" a respectable meaning.

I faithfully attended classes three times a week, learning that shoulder blades were called scapulas, rubbing was called effleurage, kneading was called petresage, and lightly hitting the body was called tappotment. At the end of two months I took the test given by the state asking for every major bone and muscle's name and function. Then I gave the instructor a massage and graduated.

Two weeks later I received my diploma in the mail and with it the confidence to go into business for myself. I had cards printed and drove around town putting them up on every public display board I could find. I also put an ad in a newspaper for the first and last time and my name in the phone book under "massage." As a result, for the next four years I had calls at all hours of the night. These callers panted lewd suggestions in my ear.

After all my effort I had three massages the first Saturday I was in business. My first client was a man who wanted me to come to his home in the Hollywood Hills. I got a map and found my way. I was nervous. I wasn't sure this man believed me when I told him I did "therapeutic" massage. What if he wanted sex? He was a stranger. He would be nude. It is one thing massaging a naked friend under a blanket or a fellow student or someone in a spa. Doing "out-calls" is a different story.

When I found the house where I was to give my first massage as an independent, official, licensed and certified masseuse the driveway was so steep there was no way I could drive up it or carry my massage table. I walked to the door, bottle of oil and towel in my hand and knocked.

After considering the situation, we decided not to haul the table up the driveway. We agreed I would massage him on his bed. Inside I thought of my beautiful new table with the bridge suspension legs sitting in the backseat of my car.

The man I massaged moaned throughout the whole treatment. Every time I massaged his leg, his penis would flap around like a fish dying on the shore, out of sight beneath the terry cloth blanket my mother had hemmed by hand.

He paid me $25, and I was off to my second massage. This man worked on an oil rig and was in town for the weekend. He was huge and very annoyed because I didn't want him to massage me. My third client was a man who never stopped smiling at me seductively, his gold teeth glinting in the half-light.

I came home with $75 and a leaden heart. I had a vision of what I would be for people. I wanted to bring love to my clients, not sex. Comfort not lust. It was a very old pain. All I had ever wanted was to inspire goodness in others. But I had never known a man, not even my father, who had not desired me sexually. Instead of getting angry, I blamed myself. What was wrong with me? What energy did

I put out that attracted this? It was thoughts like these that made my heart ache.

Another man called in response to my ad in the phone book. He called around dinnertime once or twice a week to ask if I'd beat him. We'd chat and I'd say, "No, I don't do that." Once he said I seemed so nice that he had decided to try a regular massage, but I refused.

I went out every day to let people know about my business. I went to beauty parlors and left my card. I talked to hairdressers and offered them a cheaper rate for every client they found me. I talked to waitresses and offered them discounts. I went to all the major hotels in town. They all started sending me business. But none of it was steady.

One day while I was out trying to drum up business, I went to a country club. The club offered me a room for free to massage its members. The room was in the basement, next to the lockers, which banged and clattered every time someone used them ruining the peaceful massage I was giving. It was a horrible space, drafty, noisy and cold. A month later the pipes broke, and I did a massage sloshing around in water up to my ankles. I said, "I've had it," and walked out, informing the manager that I was quitting.

That night I was so angry that I demanded from the universe a clientele made up of women in a place that was warm and dry. If these demands weren't met, I would do something else.

Two days later I got a call from Ted, the owner of a beauty parlor where I had left my card. His regular masseuse was sick, and he asked if I would like to fill in for a while. It was one of the most elite salons in Beverly Hills and I jumped at the chance to work there.

Ted's masseuse never did come back. So I began working four days a week at the beauty parlor and two afternoons a week at the health spa where I had gotten my first job as a massage therapist. In between appointments in those places I would race to someone's home for an "out-call", or to my house where I had set up a room just for massage.

I was not an instant hit at the beauty parlor. All the women who came to the shop loved their old masseuse. They simply did not want to try me. "I didn't look strong enough, I was too young, I was too thin." So the owner put an ad in the paper for cellulite massage to draw new people.

I read volumes about cellulite. I xeroxed a picture of a body to write measurements on and studied what one should eat to lose weight. I began beating peoples' bottoms and thighs to a pulp. Cellulite massage was not my idea of bringing the mind and soul and breath of life into the body, but it was paying the rent.

I asked the ladies from the country club to come to me at the beauty parlor, and when the beauty parlor ladies saw I had honest-to-goodness clients, they began using me too. I soon had more work than I could possibly handle.

A woman named Joan came to me in the beauty parlor for a regular massage and for some advice about losing weight. I gave her the first massage she had ever had. After my treatment she was so relaxed that she had trouble driving. Fearing for her safety, she asked if next time I would massage her at her home.

So every Wednesday night at eight I arrived at the entrance to her estate and rang the bell from my car. The gate would fly open, and I would enter a whole new world. Statues lined the driveway, banners flew from flagpoles, flowers grew everywhere, and a Jacuzzi gurgled next to the large swimming pool. Joan's very thin husband always met me at the door and insisted on carrying my table up the stairs, for which I was grateful.

It was a shock for me to be in the home of a truly wealthy person. Joan had a closet just for shoes. The heels hung on the wall, suspended from wooden strips to keep them from falling. They were all arranged according to color.

I never knew a person with so many shoes. Joan had never known a person with so many strange ideas. We were fascinated with each other from the start. I was a New Age massage therapist in southern California in the 1970s, and I was into everything from mucusless diets to wheatgrass enemas.

I don't know if it was her work as a writer or her inherent curiosity, but through Joan I discovered what a storyteller I was. She could pull stories out of me quicker than anyone I'd ever met. In fact, before meeting Joan, I didn't have the faintest idea I knew so much. In no time she knew everything I knew about pressure points in the feet and their relation to all the organs in the body. She knew what I thought about religious cults and who joined them, my personal stories about Sai Baba, Kirpal Singh, and Ram Dass; what I had read about food combining, lecithin and garlic capsules; my life as a hippie; how breast feeding develops both sides of a baby's brain; how to heal cancer through macrobiotics, colonics and so forth.

After six months of getting massage Joan began to open up herself. She had lost at least forty pounds as a result of my pounding, her restraint, and the marvels of lecithin, garlic, and lots of water. Then she began to break down emotionally.

Through Joan I saw, for the first time, how unresolved conflict is expressed in the body. How the body, in fact, acts out our core beliefs. And when we go against these beliefs, there is hell to pay. Underneath all that weight and tension lived Joan's fear of her softness, vulnerability and feminine power.

I could not have been more pleased for her emotional release. I had finally found someone who would work with me in the way I wanted to work. Joan, on the other hand, thought she was losing her mind. I would walk into her beautiful bedroom and set up my table, then she would lie down and sob. What came up was her mother. Joan's mother had trained her to honor her intelligence.

Somehow her mother had relayed that it was cheap to have an attractive body. When Joan lost all that weight and became a beauty, the war began. One minute she was raging about the stupid ideas her mother had planted in her head; the next she was grieving about all the ways she hated herself.

After an emotional outpouring, Joan would be embarrassed. I tried to convince her that nothing she could do would lower the esteem I had for her, but she didn't believe me. She was ashamed. She wanted to leave the past behind. There was nothing I could do. She had lost the weight she wanted. She was fitting into size eight jeans. She looked terrific and she stopped calling. I missed her terribly.

Whenever a client stopped seeing me, I felt deserted. I knew things about my clients that their husbands or close friends didn't know, but we weren't friends. We were something else. I was taken into the very center of a person's world but allowed only to look. After a massage was over, I returned to my world, void of the intimacy of that family. Massage is a strange kind of intimacy. I may know a person's most intimate secrets, but I don't know their facades.

Watching Joan struggle through her problems with "mother" brought up my own issues. I was fascinated at seeing the intricacies of Joan's upbringing. In this way I began to look into my own psyche, at things I had never really thought about.

After a session with Joan I would drive slowly home or stop by the beach and walk along the sand, contemplating and crying about my past, which was still so vague. My mother was afraid of her own beauty and of attracting attention. She did not know how to keep my father (not that anyone could)—who was a restless, sensual man —at home. Someone would invariably tell her they had seen my father with a woman they thought at first was her. Sometimes husbands would come to the house asking Mom if Dad had been out on such and such a night. Mom would grow resentful, moody and silent. She would go for days without talking to either of us while Dad was having an affair. During this time of her despair Dad and I stayed close.

Later Mom would be jealous of my closeness with Dad and tell him things to make him angry at me. She would turn an event into something horrible like my climbing to the top of our neighbor's forty-foot fig tree, or dancing wildly to the organ in church. She would hound him, telling him if he didn't punish me, I would end up lawless and outrageous, just like Aunt Grace. She would threaten to leave him if he didn't spank me. She would stand behind the door while Dad would sit with me on the bed trying to gather the courage to do what she demanded so he could win his way back into her heart. Sometimes Dad and I would pretend. He would hit the bed, and I would yell my head off .

When Dad finally found a woman he wouldn't stop seeing, Mother left him for good. The day she served him with divorce papers I was eleven years old. We stayed with friends, out of town, so he could collect his things. The next morning when we returned, Dad had taken everything but our clothes and my bed. Our house was completely bare, as though no one lived there. On my pillow was a note from him. It read, "I will always love you."

6

Smoke

IT USED TO BE I couldn't be with anyone, man or woman (especially people I admired), without becoming self-conscious and shy. Being a masseuse got me past that. I had a role, a purpose and a routine that gave me a way of being. My contact with a client lasted only an hour. If I told a story and didn't get a response like "Um hum" or "That reminds me of" or "Ain't it the truth," I knew to be quiet.

I found I had a lot to say when massaging. When I began to massage a client, the walls of fear and insecurity that kept me isolated began to melt. It was easy for me to talk with the heat of my clients coming up through my hands. The warmth of their bodies reassured me. Even now when I have something difficult to say to someone, I ask, "Can I massage you?"

Sometimes my clients and I just listened to music. Sometimes we were silent, and I would massage them until they asked a question like "Well, what happened next?" Or "Did she find out who he was having an affair with?" Or "What do you think about face-lifts?" Or "Did they ever find that boat?" There were stories I told and stories I didn't, and many got mixed up because there were parts of them I could tell and parts I didn't want anyone to know about.

One of the stories I told my clients when they wanted to quit some bad habit was how I quit smoking. I began by telling them what a glorious habit this was for me, and how I discovered cigarettes when I was sixteen. I loved cigarettes from the first moment I took smoke into my lungs. I loved the sensation of lighting the cigarette, blowing out the match, sucking, inhaling, holding my breath, exhaling and tapping the ash. I loved the way cigarettes gave me something to do when I hadn't the faintest idea of what to do. I loved how smoking gave me something wordless to do with people. I loved the way it took my white, blue-eyed, blond-hair, Grace Kelly look and gave the world the impression that I had a black leather jacket waiting for me in my closet.

I loved the way smoking seemed to burn a hole in my ozone and gain attention from all those dangerous boys on motorcycles who had ignored me before. I loved the way my mother hated my smoking, the panic that would rise in her voice when she caught me. Through my smoking I could say, "I don't care about you, Mom," in a brand new language.

I was addicted to smoking in no time. Countless times over the next twelve years I tried to quit smoking. During my last year in high school, I tried to quit smoking when I played Anna in *The King and I* so that I could sing better. I tried to quit smoking for my husband, who said he wouldn't marry me unless I did. But I smoked in my wedding dress after walking down the aisle and in the bathroom at the reception hall. I tried to quit when I was pregnant with Russell, and I tried to quit each day of the whole eight months I nursed him, just "not today, not today." I tried to quit smoking when I became a hippie and ran a health food restaurant in Boston. But I was still smoking when I went into the convent in 1975.

I had not been behind the convent walls for ten minutes before I had a nicotine attack. I wanted a cigarette so badly I thought I would die. I didn't want it as badly then as I wanted it later that night, though. I lay in bed after an hour of silence, dinner, two hours of classes, an hour of meditation on my knees—in which God was a deep drag I couldn't have, the Marlboro man I could never reach—and evening prayers.

Everyone in the convent went to bed at eleven. I listened for all the sounds in the house to stop. When all was quiet, I got out of bed and crept toward my cigarettes, which were hidden in a special pocket of my black purse. I heard the breathing of the other women in the room while I pulled a cigarette from my purse. Then I found some matches used to light candles and snuck down two flights of stairs to the basement. There I knew I could light my cigarette without being detected. When I pulled the smoke into my lungs I fell to the floor. I simply collapsed from the rush of nicotine through my veins. Even though I was down and could barely move, I still got the cigarette to my mouth. Yes, I was an addict. I snuck cigarettes in the convent for nine months. Almost my entire stay.

At one point while in the convent, I had to go to the dentist. There in the waiting room was a book called *How To Find Your Soul Mate*. I read it in fifteen minutes, though it was clearly not on the prescribed reading list for nuns. The author described in detail how to attract the mate of one's dreams by daily repeating a statement describing the type of person one wanted. He said this daily repetition would draw one's mate through magnetism. He suggested one be as specific as possible, choosing a time and date for this meeting.

I decided to test this theory out on the impossible task of quitting smoking. That very day I created my cigarette affirmation: "On November 8th at midnight I will no longer smoke cigarettes, for the raising of my consciousness and the health of my entire being in accordance with God's divine law, and with the help of all the saints and sages of all ages, Amen." I wasn't taking any chances of offending anyone. November 8th was three months away, which made me feel comfortable. Maybe it would never arrive. Maybe I would die and I wouldn't have to quit.

But of course I didn't die and the day came. On the evening of November 8th, 1975, I smoked my brains out until midnight. The next day I awoke and had no desire for a cigarette at all. In fact, quitting was a relief. Finally, I could stop repeating the affirmation.

When I became a masseuse, I told this story to everyone who wanted to change anything. But I left out a lot. I left out the fact that I was a nun when I quit. I left out the fact that I had been in a foster home when I started smoking—a home where my mother sent me when I became a wild person she could not control. I just gave my clients the bare bones of the story.

Years later I wrote an article about using affirmations; the process of repeating what one wants over and over. The article was called "Affirmation Backfire." In it I described how everything I got through repeating affirmations brought with it things I didn't want, too. For instance, instead of smoking I now had a coffee addiction I couldn't get rid of, and when I later did affirmations for a soul mate and asked for someone who was tall, he came along, but he was six foot five, which was ridiculous for my height. He was also so beautiful I was jealous the entire time I was with him, and he smoked so much dope I thought he was an addict. Because of my three months of saying the affirmation for this man, I became so bonded it was impossible to get away from him. I was tied to him for eight miserable years.

I told the whole story about doing my "soul mate affirmation" in the article, the point of which was to enjoy and love whatever situation you found yourself in, but no matter. All the mail I received from people who read the article was for more information about how they too could find a soul mate."

I learned a lot about human nature through telling my clients this story. Everyone I told this story to, and to my knowledge those who read my article, didn't have the discipline or didn't want the same thing for three months. I guess one has to be desperate. I believe it is the state of longing that creates the "burning bush," whether it is a mate, a home, or quitting a habit that is killing you. I have been surprised to find that most people are terrified to want anything, to make a mistake, or even to get what they want.

7

Mrs. Adams

A WOMAN NAMED MRS. ADAMS came for massage in the beauty parlor. She was in her eighties and didn't see well. She also couldn't turn her head because of a stiff neck. Because of this she couldn't park her car. She'd bang into everything; the car in front, the car behind, the curb. So once a week, I went to her house, carrying my massage table and all my things (sheets, oil, blankets and pillows) up the stairs to her second story condo. She lived there with her husband, to whom she'd been married for 65 years, and a black cat named Farley.

Getting up the stairs was the first of many obstacles to overcome before my massage with Mrs. Adams could begin. Getting someone to open the door was the second. Mrs. Adams was as slow as winter in Maine, and Mr. Adams was deaf. I'd bang away on the door with both fists. The doorbell never worked.

Once inside with my table set up, Mrs. Adams would come in and I'd help her take off her girdle. We had a routine. She would put her hands on my shoulders, I would pull the girdle off her hips and down her legs. Then I'd give her my arm so she could step out of it safely where it lay on the floor like a flat tire.

To get her on the table, I boosted her up where she collapsed in a heap. Next I straightened her out, pulling on her arms and legs in which muscle tone was merely a memory. Then I lifted her shoulders and hips so her flesh could rearrange itself and settle in comfort.

I often wondered how skin as thin as hers could hold the blood. It did an imperfect job at best. Purple marks told of her bumping into walls and doors or perhaps her desk.

Mrs. Adams liked to keep the shades open to let in the sunlight. Once I mentioned that people across the way might see her. This old, proper, southern woman who had every pillow case and sheet in the linen closet wrapped in its own tissue paper, said, "If they see something they've never seen before, they can throw a shoe at it." This bit of openness was the only discrepancy I ever noticed in this otherwise proper, private, secretive woman.

I think her own body was a secret to her. Once while I was hoisting her up on the table, she caught a glimpse of herself in the mirror, naked. Her breasts fell down to her stomach, saggy bags of empty skin. Her stomach and every inch of her was wrinkled and hanging off the bone. She stopped and stared at herself. I was anxious and felt the need to protect her from the sight.

"Is that me?" she asked.

I felt too awkward to answer. Suddenly, she burst out laughing.

"What a mess," she said with a sigh.

Though their home was filled with luxury there was a sense of death there, of things decaying and of secrets. Mrs. Adams never told "Papa" the constant pain she was in or that she was dying of cancer. "It would have frightened him," she said.

She also told me that she knew Papa was losing his mind, but she never said a word to him. Instead she set out his checks each week for him to sign because he would not have remembered, and she made secret phone calls to their broker in order to take charge of their money.

Mr. Adams, who had run a business all his life, knew government secrets, and once had hundreds of people working for him, did not know his wife read the *Wall Street Journal* in the bathroom each day so she could look after their investments.

The Adams had outlived most of their friends and all but one 300-pound son who had moved away. One look at him told me what growing up in this land of secrets had been like. He had buried himself alive with food to keep away the horrible feelings of emotional starvation.

This cloud of secrets affected me, too. When I walked through those doors, I left everything about me that was sexual, alive, intelligent, moist, deep, feline, healing or original at the door. In Mrs. Adams' presence I couldn't remember that I'd read *The Tibetan Book Of The Dead*, Carl Jung, or Dostoyevsky.

But I learned a great deal from Mrs. Adams, and I enjoyed our "visits," as she called them. I learned a different kind of closeness through her, which had nothing to do with agreeing with each other. It was closeness born of words not said. There was a part of me that understood her sighs, a look, a moment's hesitation, all of which made me love her. I knew for certain I was the only one who saw that look of despair or heard that sigh, and I would have lugged my table up five flights of stairs to give her an hour's comfort. I knew her at her dying time, when all the wisdom she had gained from her life's experiences had been melted down to its essence, when all her endurance, discipline and courage shone in her eyes.

She had the will of a road warrior. She told me that she had allowed herself one cigarette along with one cocktail every day with her husband at 4:00 P.M. for 65 years.

She said her maid used to say, "There they are, courting again."

I asked, "Didn't you ever want another cigarette or another drink?"

"Oh, yes," she said, "sometimes I wanted one very badly."

Mrs. Adams told me things she had never told another soul. She told me things like; "I never got to ride a bicycle. My parents were poor. Our maid drinks." I wish I'd heard her say just once, "I'm dying of cancer and I'm scared."

After four years of massaging her weekly, she had to stop. It was just too painful for her to get up on the table. The last time I saw Mrs. Adams was after Papa died. She called to tell me and I went to see her. I walked into her exquisite living room where I saw the wallpaper falling down in sheets. Her cataracts made it impossible for her to see it.

There was a chair Mrs. Adams had in her sitting room that I had always loved. Farley had clawed the arms to shreds. The scene made me want to steal everything. At that moment I understood a scene from the movie, *Zorba the Greek*. When the foreign woman died, all the women in the village descended on her house and stripped it to the bone. The women were like furies. They took down her curtains and fought over her shawls, opened the closets and took her slips and stockings, her umbrella, her parrot and her dresser. What they couldn't carry down the stairs they threw over the balcony. Standing in Mrs. Adam's living room, I understood that scene; it was a shout declaring, "I am alive. I still have needs. I am alive. I want."

I never saw Mrs. Adams again. When I went back six months later, no one by that name lived there. I tried to find out what had become of her. I talked to the man who opened the gate for visitors and the manager, but no one knew anything. I felt terrible that I had not come back to visit her sooner. How had so much time slipped away? But then it took time to know how much she meant to me, how her words, her gestures, her stories, had crept into my psyche and taken up residence in my body.

One very late, cold November night, on my way home from massaging a businessman, speeding down Sunset in my beat up old Honda, massage table in the hatchback, I suddenly knew she was dead. I became aware in a flash of all she had given me; a model of dignity and discipline to contain her desires in a way my family never did.

There in the car I cried for her and I cried for myself, and I cried for all the women whose upbringing could not let them say, "I have cancer and I'm scared, Papa. Hold me in your mad arms, and help me bear it."

When I am feeling very old and tired, Mrs. Adams enters my mind and stares at me with her watery, gray eyes, so filled with compassion and pain. She gave me a vision of strength and courage to endure all that life brought - to the very end.

8

Hoover

I WAS POUNDING Pam's cellulite in the massage room of an exercise studio, another place I worked for a while. Instructors shouting, "Kick right, kick left, tighten thighs, breathe," came through the walls. Such frantic energy, such loud noise and so much effort expended to use up the excesses of affluence: too much money, food, time, cars; not enough sex, love or dignity. My back hurt. I wanted to fart. I was feeling sorry for myself.

Just that morning I had been to the doctor. I had a pelvic inflammatory infection many years before and I thought it had come back. While examining me the doctor said I would never get pregnant again. He told me no more eggs would make it through my mangled fallopian tubes. All those potential children who could show me a different part of myself would die without a breath, without a cry or sound, without limbs or insight or wisdom or anger. I could stop making marks on the calendar.

I was bemoaning my fate when Pam said, "What you need, honey, is a puppy."

When I finished the massage, we headed straight for the pound. We looked in cages at dogs of all sizes. Then a volunteer walked by with an eight-week-old, furry, fuzzy, cuddly black puppy with four white feet and a white chest. He fit in both hands and was the only one in a litter of eight who hadn't found a home. He had arrived at the pound that afternoon. He was a Sagittarius, but at the moment he did not look much like a philosopher. He was bewildered and had funny ears that flopped when he walked. I called him Mr. Floppy Ears until his real name came to me; Hoover. He was not named after the dam or the president but after the vacuum cleaner because he ate everything on the floor.

The first morning of Hoover's life with me a woman came to my house for massage. I put Hoover in the kitchen and closed the door. He began to whine and yap, pressing his black nose under the door, trying to get a whiff of me. Well, of course he got in and took up residence under my table, where he lay during every massage I did at home for the next thirteen years.

Hoover was the main reason I worked at home. I remember when I took a full time job in a facial salon. Every day while I was at work, Hoover took everything he could get his teeth on in the garage, carted it out to the driveway and tore it to shreds. After three days of this I got the message, quit my job and came home where I belonged.

When I massaged someone in their home, Hoover came along and sat on my client's shaded front porch or under a tree with a bowl full of water and waited for me. Unleashed, he would wait for hours. He would not tolerate being tied up unless he was in a public place where he might be mistaken for a stray. And there were lots of places I chose not to go because I couldn't take Hoover with me.

He was quiet as a mouse under my table. He knew scratching and licking were not allowed. If he had to do such things, he left the room. Sometimes when I was massaging, he put his head on my foot, a gesture of friendship and devotion.

Hoover was a great teacher of mine. Even when he was very old, blind and deaf, with arthritis in his back, he communicated with me through signs, the language of dogs. When I heard him pant, I knew his water bowl was dry. There was a certain look that meant, "Take me for a walk," and another that said, "You forgot my dog bone." There were times he let me know he needed to run wild or rummage through trash to remember he was really a wolf, and times he needed to be on a leash to keep him safe from being picked up and taken back to the pound, or to keep him with me in large crowds. He taught me the language of grunts, tail wags, side steps and squeals. He had a way of licking his lips to ask for a bite.

Sometimes I would get angry with Hoover when he didn't do what I wanted fast enough. It was usually because I hadn't taken the time to be clear or make sure he was listening. Anger with him was always a mistake. When he knew what I wanted, he always tried to comply out of his love for me, not fear. Fear of me made Hoover a coward. It made him sneaky and resentful. At these times, when I'd been bad, I had to sit with him a long time, scratching his ears and his favorite place on his back, or rubbing his tummy, or just sitting with him quietly. He was always forgiving. If I carried on too long, he got up and left in disgust.

Because I did not get to raise my son, there was incompleteness in me that had to be filled by a similar task. Taking care of Hoover completed that task. It was difficult keeping a dog in L.A. Some places I lived didn't take dogs. I had to hide him when the manager came by. I had to walk him four times a day so he could get his exercise and be comfortable. The last year and a half of his life he was sick, needing medication and special care. I performed these acts as though he were my child. Through Hoover I proved to myself that I could go to the end with something. I proved to myself that I could endure and that someone could not only survive, but also thrive under my care. I proved to myself that I could be faithful and that I could love.

After fifteen years of being my familiar, he died on a camping trip with me in the Rocky Mountains of Colorado. He died in my arms, his furry face next to mine. When my friends found out about his death, I received fifty condolence letters. One man wrote to me, "Watching you and Hoover was like watching one of the great loves of the world; like Hepburn and Tracy, Anthony and Cleo."

I took his ashes with me back to California. My mother, Russell and I did a ceremony for him. We went into the woods, sat around his box of ashes, and told "Hoover stories." Then we scattered his ashes, crying our eyes out.

9

Sam and Babe

THE ONLY LEGITIMATE CALL I ever got from my ad in the phone book was from Sam and Babe. Sam was a retired rock star, and Babe was an ex-hair dresser and now Sam's gorgeous wife.

They bought a house while I knew them. It was the first house Babe had ever owned and I watched her turn it into paradise itself. She could turn a broken mirror into a beautiful, intricately patterned decoration. I watched her build a seventy-five foot by seven-foot stone wall along one side of their property, all decorated with the ends of wine bottles. She planted cactus gardens that looked as if she had been to design school. She had amazing vision. Her walkways sprouted arbors, sweet peas crawling up and over them, laughing and waving red, lavender, purple and white blossoms. She could plan a stairway in her head, create a wall of mirrors and design a patio with a fountain before I'd finished massaging her feet. Once, after a massage, she gave me a jar of homemade moisture cream she'd made from avocados and cucumbers she'd grown from seeds.

Sam watched her creative antics and grinned. When he got bored, he would hire a plane to take them to Vegas, Europe or Bali. They came back with rolls of film. She developed the pictures and put them in albums edged with pictures from last year's calendars, sending copies to farmers and natives she'd met along the way.

For Sam's thirty-fifth birthday he and Babe invited me and six other couples to Maui, all expenses paid, to help him celebrate.

It was to be a party to end all parties. Every drug known to the Western world made it past those dogs at the airport.

I had never used cocaine before. My life was already full of things to resist. I knew I had to resist seminars and gurus with long beards and hypnotic eyes. Gurus had convinced me to give away everything I owned—twice—and I was onto them. I'd learned to resist lunch for laughs with old lovers. I'd learned to resist saying, "I'm leaving," to make a point, and coffee before bedtime. I'd learned to resist the open road, and the idea that it would all be better in Oregon, and I now resisted Double-Dutch frosted chocolate cake on sunny afternoons when I thought nothing could depress me.

In the past when I'd been offered cocaine, I had said, "No, thank you." But in Hawaii, on a warm, balmy night, in a dining room we had to ourselves, right on the water, with twelve other people doing it, and waiters tooting lines right off plates on the table, I said, "Oh, what the hell."

I had a line of coke and became addicted.

When we got back to California, Sam and Babe gave me cocaine as a tip for massage. The cocaine sang to me like a siren until it was gone. Anytime Sam and Babe called, I'd go, and from time to time I'd just show up. I tried to tie myself to the mast of sanity with thoughts of caution, fear and incriminations. Then I remembered what Henry Miller wrote about one of his characters: "He didn't believe in moderation nor good sense nor anything that was inhibitory. He believed in going the whole hog and then taking his punishment." Perhaps Henry Miller had a sense of self that allowed him to have confidence and dignity even with his head in the toilet.

I'd go out on a limb with my head full of "Millerisms" or some borrowed ideology that said, "Live life to the fullest," then come crashing down with no inner confidence to support such thoughts. I could go "the whole hog," but I couldn't take the punishment the drugs dished out. The highs would lead to the lows, and the lows would make me crave the highs again, and eventually the cycle would lead me to despair and anxiety attacks. When I took drugs or drank too much, I didn't know what I thought or felt or whether it was I or the drugs talking. I needed a middle path, a harbor, a safe port, shallow warm water that was quiet and calm so that I could begin to hear the faint sound of my Self again.

I got to a point where I couldn't tell which voice in my head was telling me the truth. The only thing that kept me going was massaging my clients. Mrs. Adams kept me alive, along with Mrs. Crow, Mrs. Cook, Mrs. Douglas, Mrs. Vanderbilt, Mrs. Earl, and the general's wife, the soap opera writer and all the others. As soon as I lay my hands on their bodies, whatever was going on with me would fade into the background, and I would be at peace. I saw most of my clients every week. I usually had six appointments a day. I loved them. They loved me. They gave me birthday presents and extra money at Christmas. I never came to them drunk or stoned. They were my shrine, my offering, and my prayer. I never wanted to pollute them.

Each morning I awoke and drank a liver flush, which consisted of fresh orange juice, a lemon, garlic and olive oil. After yoga and meditation I went to work. When I came home, after talking all day about the importance of diet, relaxation and self-cleansing, I would smoke a cigarette, drink a glass of wine, and snort a line of cocaine off the mirror that lived under the sofa and hope no one called.

When Russell came to visit for the summer, I stopped doing everything: smoking, drinking, cocaine. I repeated affirmations to clean up my act, starting a month in advance of Russell's arrival. When Russell came for the summer he and I lived at the beach. I watched him ride the waves on his boogie board, his white East Coast body would turn golden brown, and the tension in his face caused by school and his drive to become a star athlete would relax.

One summer, however, I found I couldn't stop drinking. During this time, I met a woman who taught re-evaluation counseling. I took her course. One of her exercises was to tell another person in the group our life story. Then the other person would tell their story. Telling my life story in an hour I heard myself say many times, "My life began to fall apart as I was drinking too much."

Soon after this class I took another workshop to become a rebirther. Rebirthing is a technique used to clear up birth trauma.

The workshop was held every evening for several weeks in the large living room of one of the participants. One evening we went around the room and each person was given the chance to talk about what the workshop had done for them, and I heard myself say, "It has given me a place to come every night so I wouldn't have to drink."

The words were out before I could catch them. They were like wild birds, or bats let out from a dark cave. Blind, they darted about the room, their wings beating the air hysterically. In the silence, which was filled with fear, remorse, pity, mercy, compassion and benevolence, someone asked, "Are you an alcoholic?" And I said, "Yes, yes I am."

It was more than a year before I could stop drinking and using drugs. Just admitting my addiction to sixty people wasn't enough. I had to reach complete and utter defeat. It was like crawling down into the bowels of the earth, where I would beg and bargain and plead with the gods of the underworld to let me have just one more night with my beloved. The beloved who would lead me to feelings of union, where I could live out my fantasies in peace. Where I could feel I was a great soul chained, like Prometheus, to the rock of despair. And all was romantic, not tragic.

In the evening after work when the drug or wine wore off , I would go to the bathroom and wash my hands and mouth, put on cold cream and get into bed, praying for sleep. Sometimes I got up five or six times a night and went through my routine: up and down the driveway, drinking, washing, cleansing, doing cocaine, feeling calm or anxiety, finding the matches, one more cigarette left.

I remembered my Aunt Grace, who came to live with Mom and me every time she got a divorce. I remembered hearing my Aunt, seeing light under her door, the smell of her cigarette coming through the heating vent, the quiet foot steps down the hall to the kitchen, the squeak of the cupboard door where the liquor was kept. Sometimes I would hear her cry. She died at forty-five of liver disease. Had her ghost entered me? Was I walking her hall, performing her ritual, reaching the end for both of us? Perhaps I wasn't trying to escape my life. Maybe I was being a loyal servant to the dead.

Eventually I reached the bottom of the pit. It happened one night when I was at a party with all my healing friends. Everyone was outside in the hot tub under a starry sky. Candles accented the landscaped patio, and little lanterns gave light to a path lined with huge oak trees. I walked through the kitchen and living room drinking every half-filled glass of beer, wine, whiskey, and vodka—even the ones with cigarettes put out in them. When I was through and there was not a drop of liquor left in the house, I realized I was stone sober.

It reminded me of a time I took a hit of acid and nothing happened. Then I took another hit. A minute later the first hit came on so strong it took my head off. I realized then that the second tab hadn't even hit my stomach. There was a moment of clarity. Right before I went off to other worlds, when I knew I had taken on much more than my nervous system had ever dealt with, and there was no way out but through the asshole of the universe, there was only time to think, "OOPS."

I awoke in my bed at three in the morning wondering how I got there. I could not move, or the creatures right before my eyes would have pounced on me. They were circling me with their rat eyes, making me hold still. I could hear them at my throat and deep inside my guts, sucking, gnawing, hissing.

I had hallucinations for three days before I was able to call my friend Annette, who told me about a group of people who could help me. I was ready. I would do anything not to repeat that experience of anguish, fear and despair. And from that night in 1980 I stopped all use of drugs or alcohol, and, by the grace of God, have not gone back to them.

And I let go of my clients Sam and Babe. Just hearing their voices on the phone made me want cocaine. I was afraid to see them, afraid that in their presence I would lose my resolve to stop using drugs. I came to the realization that sometimes in order to let go of the worst of life; the best goes with it.

10

Massage of the Heart

SWEDISH MASSAGE is "massage of the heart." To give one is an act of love. It is caring for that person as if they were your own beloved. At times my clients' little fingers are as dear to me as my son's. Their aching backs become my mother's; their feet, my guru's. When I've reached that point of love within myself, I feel I have connected with the God in us both. It is an act of communion and takes sinking into the silence to get there. It is rare to find someone who can be that still. During massage, when getting close to deep silence, people will frequently leap up or say something desperate or simply fall asleep. But sometimes it happens that both of us get to that place of indescribable stillness, and we are able to feel the magic of connection and become one, floating in the vastness of being.

In the past, after a week of massaging, I often couldn't flex my hands, and sometimes I couldn't talk. My mind was a jumble; my feelings a mishmash of all the people I'd worked on. Someone might come to me with a headache, and I could feel it come up my arms as I massaged her neck. She would leave feeling great, but I would have her migraine for three days.

It took me years to learn how *not* to take on my client's problems. Before I learned, my knuckles would ache from arthritis, and my back would go out on a regular basis. A chiropractor showed me how to "block" my hips, which temporarily adjusted and relieved my back. This technique consisted of lying on my stomach and putting a block of wood under each hip, which allowed my pelvis and lower back to sink into the proper position. To accomplish this on my own, I carried a pair of high-heeled shoes in my sheet and oil bag so I could block myself after each massage.

After working all day (sometimes until late at night), I would wash and hang my massage sheets. If I didn't wash them right away, or if I put them in a dryer, the almond oil I used for massage would turn rancid and the sheets would smell. So I hung them on a clothesline in the backyard. Feeling my way in the dark, a bag of clothespins around my neck, I hung the sheets so straight that they dried without a wrinkle. Sometimes I sat on the stairs beneath the sheets thinking of them collecting the essence of the night, the light of the moon and stars, and how the bright, hot sun would rise up in the morning and dry them into white flags.

When I was exhausted I would go to a stream near Ojai and put up a tent. I listened to the water and watched the way the light came through the leaves of the large oaks. I had never been so happy. I had never been so busy or felt so needed. I had never dreamed that I would be so useful to so many people or so loved. I had never dreamed there could be a life in which I fit so well.

I had been working since high school at all sorts of things. I had so many jobs I couldn't count them all. In high school I had a job as a file clerk during the summer at a title company; it took them months to find anything after I left. I had worked in the complaint department of a condominium management company. People would call when the gardeners mowed up their welcome mats, or they found a frog in their toilet, or their roof leaked. I had been a waitress in a coffee shop on the early morning shift. Once I worked as a nurse's aid, first working in a retirement home and then working in a delivery room. I had been a devoted disciple of an Indian guru, and a hippie in a commune that started the first health food restaurant in Boston.

I never wanted to be a masseuse. I never wanted to be a file clerk either, or a waitress or a secretary. I never wanted to be a nurse's aide wiping old people's bottoms and bathing what was left of their bodies, watching them as they slowly went insane from medication and neglect. I never wanted to be a nun either—I loved sex too much; I loved life too much. I never wanted to be a wife to a workaholic or a mother to a son I abandoned or alone without money, drunk. These are not things young girls' dream of being.

I'd write home to Mom, "Be patient. God isn't through with me yet." Or, "I'm collecting stories to tell my grandchildren."

My parents couldn't understand where my restlessness came from. They had moved very little. My father had the same job for forty years. Perhaps I inherited the restless genes he wouldn't use.

I believe children inherit the unresolved lives of their ancestors. On my father's side I believe I inherited his lust for pleasure and freedom. As for my mother, I believe I inherited her loneliness and her broken heart, her terror of life, and her certainty of abandonment. My mother's mother died when she was four. She was raised by resentful aunts and uncles who didn't want her and then by strangers in foster homes and orphanages. My mother had never been mothered. Now at eighty she has finally recovered and is enjoying her life. When she was sixty-eight her husband died and she sold the farm and moved to Guadalajara. She spends six months out of the year there, driving there herself. She was once held up and robbed by banditos. She mentioned it to me on page three of her weekly letter. Nothing stops her.

It took years to develop my theory of inheritance. It took one heartbreaking, out-on-a-limb adventure after another. Like the time I found myself standing in the middle of a jungle in Puerto Rico. I was looking for a man named Manuel whom I had never met. I was in a torrential rain that made noon black as night. As I stood there on a steep path turned into a stream by the rain, there was a clap of thunder that shook the earth and a flash of lightning in which I could see the pitiful predicament I was in. I had a moment of clarity. All of a sudden I realized, "I'm not paddling with both oars. I've been rendered an idiot by conflicting needs and desires which keep me in the same place."

But, by the time I'd have a thought like that, it would be too late to stop the inevitable catastrophe and I'd have to start life all over again with a new man, in a new town, looking for a new house and a new job. Its hard, even now, to stop looking for "For Rent" signs. It's become one of my "built-ins."

And for some reason, after finding a new man, a new house and a new job; after the pieces of my life began to settle I would be off again. I could not bear the anxiety that came with safety. The intensity of pain, confusion and chaos was home to me, and try as I might, I could not hold still. I moved at least fifty times in ten years. I lived in San Jose, Boston, Arlington, Cambridge, Del Mar, Roxbury, Portland and St. Petersburg. I also moved to San Francisco, Sausalito, Kennedy Meadows, Santa Barbara and Los Angeles, and many places in between.

Then by accident I became a masseuse. My clients and my profession became my refuge, a safe harbor where I could anchor my restless self. As a masseuse I could live in one town and still keep traveling from one door to the next, collecting stories, comforting clients and laughing with them. I was astonished at my good fortune in having found a job in which I got paid to touch someone. To find that I was good at something, that I had a profession I loved, a profession that supported me in a manner I had never dreamed of achieving on my own, held as much wonder for me as a miracle.

As a masseuse the separateness between body and religion began to diminish, and those two warring factions of my psyche began to merge until I saw the body as a temple, a place to worship, a holy place that houses Spirit and Soul. And I began to have confidence for the first time in my life.

And my son was proud of me.

11

Stories

EVERY CLIENT has a story that lives in my memory. I have blue stories, scarlet and magenta stories, yellow stories, black stories chartreuse and deep cobalt stories. There are stories as pale as see-through lime green and as red as blood.

I heard about affairs and sexual soirees I couldn't believe. One woman told me she had been making love in a canoe in the middle of a lake when the boat tipped over. She and her lover couldn't stop. When they finally climaxed and looked for the boat it was nowhere to be found. They never did find it. They had to swim to shore.

Riley is another story. He was a real estate man and his entire office got together and sent him to me for a massage. When he was on his back, I put one hand on his forehead and the other hand under his neck. His pulse pounded with caffeine. "How much coffee do you drink a day?" I asked.

He was amazed I knew he drank coffee. He thought I was a wizard already. "Maybe thirty cups a day," he said.

I asked him to keep track for several days and then cut the amount in half. He came back the following week and announced proudly that he was down to twenty cups. In a few months he was down to five. A few months later he gave up drinking coffee all together. This feat behind him, he discovered he hated selling real estate, that it was only large amounts of caffeine that had made it possible for him to stay at his desk and the phone for so long.

After six months Riley came to me for his last massage and told me he was moving his family to Bali where he was starting a scuba diving business. It was a lifelong dream he finally slowed down enough to remember.

12

Katherine

OVER THE YEARS, many of my clients gave me clothes. They gave me boxes full of nighties, sweaters, skirts, boots, blouses, T-shirts and swimming suits. I ended up with the most unusual wardrobe. My clients all had different styles, most of which I would never have chosen, or could not afford, and none of which went together. So what I couldn't use I passed along to friends. I opened each package with awe, as if it were buried treasure, suddenly aware of all I'd never had.

Katherine came to me for cellulite massage while I was working at the beauty shop. She was a wealthy woman who had been a debutante. When she went shopping and found something she liked, she bought it in all colors. As a result she had tons of clothes, which flowed out of her closets and drawers like lava. She gave me thousands of dollars' worth of clothes.

Katherine came to me twice a week for a year. By the time every ounce of cellulite had vanished from her thighs and buttocks, we had become very close. It was unthinkable that we should never see each other again, so we became walking buddies.

Katherine was the first client I became friends with. I never had a friend so unlike me. At first we had nothing in common except the desire to be thin and our love of walking by the ocean. As time went by, we walked every day, and every day we found more to share. As we talked, we walked faster and faster until we were doing four miles in an hour, barefoot.

We got to know each other in a whole new way. It is one thing to know someone professionally and quite another to know them privately. At first we talked about recipes for Thanksgiving and Christmas. She told me her traditions and gave me the recipe for her family's favorite pie, chocolate mousse pie, which became my son's favorite when I made it for him. In fact, I gave sugar rushes to much of the health community with Katherine's chocolate mousse pie.

I was intimidated by Katherine at first. I envied her four children and her house in the mountains. I envied her clothes, her experience as a debutante, and her wealthy beginnings. I envied her assurance in the world and the fact that she did not have to work. I loved her long fingernails, which were always polished and without chips. And I loved her hair, which always looked neat, and I loved that she drove out of town to get it trimmed. I envied her because she could wear false eyelashes without a hint of self-consciousness, and she always had a new jogging suit. I envied her Porsche, which was always clean and full of gas.

Katherine was the most feminine woman I'd ever met and cheerful as a canary. I was thirty-four and she was forty. She became the older, more mature woman in my life. I was ashamed of my life when I compared it with hers. In my eyes God loved her more than me. My mother was right; I had wasted my life.

We'd been walking for over a year and it was Christmas again. We met one morning as usual, but Katherine didn't smile when she got out of her car. She'd been crying. She was a nervous wreck. Her husband was going away on business, and he hadn't asked her to go with him. She hated him for this, and besides he wasn't leaving her enough money. What should she do? On top of that, her youngest son was in trouble. He had stolen a car, and he wouldn't go to school. He wouldn't speak to anyone in the family.

The next morning she was worse. While walking, she broke down and cried. She felt that she was losing her mind. Her family was driving her crazy. I don't believe we had ever had a silent moment between us until I realized, in the throes of her distress, that her husband was having an affair with one of my clients.

I remember my client talking about a man she loved—a man who was married and had a family. She said she was going with him to Europe over the holidays and felt guilty, but not guilty enough not to go. In one moment, as we walked in the rainbow colors the sunset reflected on the tide, it all fit together.

It was hard for me to tell Katherine. I tried to open my mouth with just a beginning word, but it was as if my body and my voice had a mind of their own. It was like they were protecting her against my will. When I was finally able to tell her, "Your husband is having an affair," our walks became dark as death. Katherine was like a tree with no roots, like a fish in air. Her philosophy did not work without money or position or a husband to give her these things.

It was a turning point for me, a recognition of myself and my value. For the first time I shared with another person how I survived a life of loss—the philosophy and knowledge I had gained while trying to make it until dawn after the loss of my son, or getting over the separation anxiety after leaving a man. I turned on my light and became Katherine's guide. I taught her to say the mantra "Divine Mother, have mercy on me." We said it together five hundred times in a row on our walks, and then she would say it in her kitchen, alone at her table.

I taught her how to listen to her breath and try to breathe with the rhythm of her heartbeat at night when she couldn't stand her thoughts. I suggested she get a notebook and write out her anger and pain as if they were a story, and to take the feelings, which were eating a hole in her belly, to bed with her and to comfort herself like a hurt child. I suggested she take those feeling of loneliness and grief and watch their passage until they settled down to the bottom of her.

And when she was totally opened by despair, we became true sisters. We had both revealed ourselves to each other. There was no fear between us. She knew everything I could remember that I had thought or done, and I knew her.

We tried to blend out lives more, but it never really worked. Katherine didn't fit into my life, and I didn't fit into hers. Her house made me uncomfortable; she never liked "long-hairs." I didn't like the relationship she had with her children or the way she treated her dogs. It was only when we walked along the beach, waves crashing, stepping through water or along the hard sand, around the points and over the rocks, always barefoot, that we were in perfect harmony.

After her divorce, Katherine moved away. We wrote Christmas cards for several years and telephoned when we needed to hear each other's voice for comfort. I often wonder if she still has need of the prayers I taught her. I wonder if her concept of life deepened from knowing me. She taught me that no matter what our position in life, no matter how much money we have, how fine our house or our clothes, in our hearts we are all the same.

I love you, Katherine, wherever you are. I hope you are well, my sister.

13

Stewart

STEWART, AN ACCOUNTANT, was the husband of a client who had purchased ten massages for him for his birthday. He didn't even want one, but he came to keep peace in his home. He arrived at my front door right on time, wearing a three-piece suit, reeking from the cares and tensions at work.

I told him what to do with his clothes, how to lie down on the table under the towel, and left him to do so in private. When I returned, he was on top of the towel in his boxer shorts, which was just fine with me.

I put one hand under his neck and one on his forehead. I felt his neck and head pulsing with tension. His skin was damp and clammy. His body odor was awful. This man was stressed to the max. I had to get rid of all my squeamishness in order to touch his smelly feet. I told him his only job now was to let go and relax. I might as well have saved my breath. Every time I touched him, he tensed. I tried to talk pleasantly about this and that—his wife, his birthday, what he did for a living. Nothing I said or did made Stewart relax or feel comfortable. He began to fidget and sigh with annoyance. It was as if I were causing him pain.

The following week he began our session with a question, "What do you think is the key to relaxation?" I thought it was a trick question; he merely wanted to find an opening to ridicule all my ideas, but I played the game. I told him, "Being at peace with your past, a good diet, and a good mental outlook."

"Well, that's pretty simplistic," he said.

At that point I was massaging his leg, which he held up in the air. Irritably I said, "Stewart, you are doing everything possible to ensure that absolutely nothing will happen here. I am trying my best to relax you and make this a pleasant experience. If you don't want a massage or don't like me, I will be happy to refund your money."

I was astonished at my outburst. I had never snarled at a client before. Silence and tension filled the room. Finally he said, "I'm sorry. I know I'm tense and irritable. That's why I'm here. I can't get along with anyone. I have promised my wife I will go to one of those weekend seminars to discover why I'm so angry. I'm going to it next weekend. Let's see if I'm better after that. Give me one more chance."

He could have blown me over with a feather.

The next week I could not believe my eyes when I opened the door to greet him. Stewart's face was filled with a mixture of aliveness, softness and strength. He gave me a hug and apologized for being so uncooperative. He said he had spent the whole weekend crying about his childhood and the resentments he had toward his parents. The wasted time. Over the weekend he had called his parents and told them his insights and asked their forgiveness for making them responsible for his miserable life. He had made amends to his wife and his stepdaughter.

When I put my hands on his body, there was not a bit of tension anywhere. It validated my belief that the body is the physical manifestation of all our thoughts and emotions. Tension is a result of negative thinking, of unexpressed feelings and unexpressed fears we don't face. It seems Stewart's tears and forgiveness had cleaned him out. If I had not felt the difference with my own hands, I would not have believed it. I did not think a person could change himself so drastically in one weekend, but Stewart was proof that change could happen quickly. From that moment on, Stewart's life continued to change. I continued to massage he and his wife for many years.

14

Jan, Muktananda & Kirpal Singh

MY FAVORITE CLIENT was a starlet named Jan. Jan and I inspired each other to expose our most outrageous stories, and we would howl with laughter. We roared and shrieked over our stories, getting more and more animated with each tale. Sometimes Jan had to relax from the sheer exhaustion of laughing.

Some people are amazed when I tell them about talking or laughing during a massage. They assume that to get the benefit of touching, a person has to be quiet. It has been my experience that people often need to talk before allowing intimacy. So the more intimate I am with my own stories, the safer another person is in sharing their stories. It isn't about the person on the table baring their soul; it is about what we create together. If I have a breakthrough about my life while I am doing a massage, my client can benefit from it too.

I don't believe I ever enjoyed massaging anyone more than Jan. I usually massaged Jan in her living room, but one day she had all her curtains out being cleaned so we decided to use the bedroom. I carried my table into her bedroom and stopped dead still. There on her dresser was a picture of Muktananda, an Indian guru I had great respect for. I said to her, "Oh, you know Muktananda? I used to have an Indian guru."

She asked, "What was his name?"

"Kirpal Singh," I said, and told her then and there the whole story.

I learned about Kirpal Singh after my divorce. I was hopelessly lost and living on the streets in Cambridge, Massachusetts, selling *The Phoenix*, and *Boston After Dark* newspapers at Harvard Square.

One day a young man who bought a paper hung around to talk. Soon the subject of spirituality came up, and he invited me to his home, where he lived with a number of others who followed the teachings of an East Indian man. I was curious and hungry, so I went that night to have dinner and hear more about this person.

There were pictures of Kirpal Singh all over the place. He wore a turban and had piercing, blue eyes that shot out of his dark face. His beard was long and gray. All in all he was the perfect looking guru.

At dinner I was told that none of Kirpal Singh's devotees ate meat or eggs and sex was not allowed except to make babies. Devotees had to meditate two hours a day and listen to something called the "sound current" for another hour. Also, no one was allowed to consume a single drop of alcohol or a tab of MDA, LSD, peyote, pot, hash, morning glory seeds, black beauties, reds, downers, arsenal cans - nothing! And with that I walked out the door.

In bed that night as I was dropping off to sleep, I thought, "What was that man's name?" Sometime during the night, as I lay fast asleep, his face suddenly stared into mine and he said, "My name is Kirpal Singh."

I sat up in bed, immediately awake. Kirpal Singh had visited me, of that I was sure. I was sure he had heard me ask his name, and somehow he had found me. I could still feel his presence in the room. I was shaken and impressed and thought, "Well, maybe I'll give his group a try."

I found out where the meditation groups met in Boston and began going several times a week. Except for a few flickering candles, we all sat in the dark. I tried to concentrate on the silence and not think of beer. To me everyone who went there seemed holy. They all seemed to have a particular, knowing smile that reeked of gratitude and well-being. I would look in the mirror and practice that smile, trying to fathom its meaning, trying to see how it felt on my face. It never felt natural. Usually I left the meditation hall and headed straight to the liquor store. Perhaps that's why I never got the smile right.

Three months later Kirpal Singh came to Boston. From the first moment I saw him I loved him. I went to hear him lecture. I couldn't understand a word he said because of his Indian accent, but I experienced a peace I had never known. He was going to give initiation to those who had been able to refrain from sex, drugs, alcohol, mayonnaise with eggs, meat, lying, cheating, etc., etc. for three months. I thought, "Maybe I can sneak in and he won't know." I was desperate to stop drinking. I was miserable at the loss of my son. I visited Russell every other weekend, and I thought, "I may not be able to have a normal life my mom could appreciate, but maybe I can rise above it all by becoming enlightened."

At the initiation ceremony Kirpal Singh went around the room touching people. When he came to me, his eyes closed, for what seemed like hours, before he touched me. He had accepted me as a student. I felt while he stood before me that he was reading my "karma"—all past mistakes and good deeds—and was deciding whether to take me on as a project. I felt he knew I hadn't done a thing according to his rules, but for some reason he didn't refuse me.

For months I said the mantra. I got up at five in the morning where ever I was, with a lover, in a car, on a train, hitch hiking to Connecticut to visit my son. I'd get up at dawn and say that mantra for two hours all wrapped up in "The Blue Cloud." I went to meditations and services in Boston where his tapes where played, and I did my best to concentrate. I kept a record of all my transgressions, which, according to the rules, I sent to Kirpal Singh every three months.

After three months, however, I was ready to give up on the whole project. Along with my daily diaries I sent a note to Kirpal Singh telling him I couldn't possibly follow all his rules and asked him to please cross me off his list. He wrote back in his shaky, eighty-two-year old hand, "Once a student is connected to the guru, you cannot be disconnected. Do not worry. Just do the best you can."

I tried to live life his way a bit longer and keep the diaries, but eventually I gave up. I later heard that Kirpal Singh had died in 1972.

Before becoming a masseuse in 1975, I went to a psychic in Los Angeles. The psychic asked, "Who is this Indian man hovering over you? He's like a mother hen to you. He loves you very much." I told her, "I can't imagine who it could be."

Since I had met Kirpal Singh, I had been in the convent and on all those drugs, which had scrambled my memory. I had forgotten all about him. I had followed many gurus. I knew the words to all of Yogananda's songs, the Indian man who had started the Self Realization Fellowship. I had been to lectures by Muktananda. I had studied with a group involved with the teachings of Gurdjieff and Ospensky. I had done mantra to Mother Mary. To each saint I prayed, "Give me back my son. Help me stop drinking. Take away this pain that lives in my heart."

Later on another psychic told me there was an Indian man whose constant prayers had saved my life. I was grateful for his help, whoever he was, but I still couldn't imagine who he might be.

Suddenly, on the day I massaged Jan in her bedroom, looking at Muktananda's picture, I knew the psychics had seen Kirpal Singh. He hadn't left me. Jan and I stared at each other. Then we both screamed and hugged and jumped up and down.

I went home from Jan's house high as a kite. I took a bath and tried to remember my mantra. It had been nine years since I'd said it. I didn't know a soul who knew about Kirpal Singh or how to contact one of his groups. I prayed to Muktananda and then to Yogananda to help me.

A friend suggested, "Why don't you go to the Bodhi Tree book store and see if someone there knows about him?" That same day I found myself on Melrose Avenue in front of the Bodhi Tree, and I walked in the door. I asked the clerk if they had a book by Kirpal Singh, and she said, "Of course."

"Well, I really don't want his book. I want to know who took over his clientele," I said.

A man standing nearby asked, "Why are you asking about Kirpal Singh?" I replied, "Because I was initiated by him many years ago. I've forgotten everything he taught me, and now I want to remember."

"Well," he said, "what do you want to know? I lived with him for six months before he died."

Hmmm.

On the wall next to us was Kirpal Singh's picture, the same one I'd seen in the house in Cambridge. Robert, the man in the bookstore, and I went outside, and on the lawn in front of the Bodhi Tree he whispered the mantra over and over until I knew it by heart. The next day Robert came to my house with books and tapes and addresses of meditation groups throughout L. A., which I went to for eight months.

But all that meditating made me crazy, the diet made me hypoglycemic, and in the end I couldn't stand the idea of another man telling me what to do with my life. What I couldn't stand the most was that little smile on the faces of all the devotees. I needed my own path. I needed to suffer to finally turn toward the light, not in despair, but in confidence that I could endure all that life brought. I had to do it my way, struggling through brambles, up and over cliff s.

There are many times I have thought, "Kirpal Singh, if I were only more obedient, if I were only less curious, how blissed out I could be. I could be saying your mantra this very minute in an ashram in Vermont with nothing more to worry about than whether to keep the snails off the tomatoes with eggshells or rows of marigolds. But, no, I had a better way. I wanted something more exciting to worry about. I wanted to see if my back would make it another year, if I would ever meet my perfect mate and husband. But

I am glad I knew you. I know we'll meet again. Thank you for coming to me and for your prayers."

I have lost track of Jan, too. I hear she lives in Canada with her husband and child. I read about her in a tabloid while waiting in line at Safeway.

15

Lola

JAN HAD A SISTER who was married to a man who used to be the husband of a wild woman named Lola, who took people to heaven through her facials. Not only did Lola's technique feel divine, it also lifted the muscles in the face causing people to look ten years younger in a single treatment—for three days. Jan said Lola was anxious to quit the facial business and move to India to live with her Guru. She was looking for someone to train for $1,000 in exchange for her knowledge and clientele. The deal sounded good to me.

Lola lived in an apartment on the beach at Malibu. When I went to her house, I could not get over the sound of the water. The Pacific Ocean was her front yard and pounded like some ecstatic, relentless god against the underpinnings of her apartment.

Lola was striking to look at. She was in her fifties, tall and blond. She had a laugh that erupted without the slightest provocation, as if she were hearing something no one else could.

There were many strange and marvelous experiences awaiting me when I entered Lola's world. Many left me a bit unnerved. First was the pink glitter she sprinkled outside her apartment entrance. In fact, Lola's whole place was pink. Her towels, the tile, her bed spread, even the pictures on the wall were pink. I'm surprised she had not sprayed the cat.

Lola had publicity pictures of all her clients arranged on one wall. For those who didn't have publicity pictures, the housewives or people not in the "biz," she would take their picture with a Polaroid camera and hang them up, too. If they were her clients, they were celebrities.

I studied her facial techniques for several months. To begin, she would put fairy music on her tape machine accompanied by hot towels bubbling in the rice cooker. With waves crashing and shaking the walls, she would work on my face. then I would work on hers, bringing fresh hot blood up the carotid artery into the neck, cheeks and forehead. There the blood fed all the cells while coursing through the veins on its way back to the heart.

One day Lola called me for a massage. I arrived at her home to find her high on acid, which, I learned, she took every month, supervised by a woman who came from Marin county. I had never heard of a supervised acid trip, but Lola did it for therapy. Lola laughed and shuddered and wept and screamed at the top of her lungs throughout the whole massage. At the end of the hour I was shaking. Afterward she leapt off the table as though nothing was the least bit out of the ordinary and handed me a check for $100. In the corner it said, "For whatever Lola wants."

She gave my name to all her clients. One woman had just wrecked her Rolls Royce while drunk. When I went to massage her, she could hardly move. I worked on her shoulders, back and feet— the parts of them that weren't bruised. As I worked on her, I told her the story of how I got sober. She was so sick she couldn't talk, so I wasn't sure what she heard. Before I left she hugged me with tears in her eyes. I began seeing her three times a week. I massaged her for the next seven years. She moved out of town, but we still sent cards and notes to each other and to my knowledge, she is still sober.

Another client referred by Lola was a beautiful woman pregnant with her third child. Toni was married to Dan, a man who built skyscrapers. I massaged this couple for nine years, every Wednesday night from eight until eleven. I don't know which of them I loved more. Dan was a riot. The first few years I massaged him, he couldn't shut up for a minute. He'd rattle on about everything, asking me questions, trying to pretend he wasn't nervous as hell about being in the nude with a woman other than Toni. He loved the way massage felt, but I could tell it made him nervous.

Getting Dan on the table without offending his dignity or invading his privacy was a comedy. I would pretend to need the bathroom so he could get on the table without me seeing him naked. Later I learned to hold the towel so he could undress behind it. Then he would lie down, and I'd drop the towel over him. Working these things out to the satisfaction of each client and their need for privacy is as much a part of the massage as anything.

Toni was just the opposite. She could walk down the hall stark naked, yelling at the kids, trying to create order out of chaos.

During the three hours I spent with them, there was a steady stream of children and animals. The children asked questions about homework, showed us pictures, tried to figure out what to wear the next day for school and discussed their teachers. Three dogs followed the children in and out and, at times took up residence under or around the table, farting like crazy. The children always gave Hoover a bone outside on the porch.

I gave up trying to teach these people anything about relaxation and psychology and decided to just love them. They screamed and abused each other in a way I had never heard before. They also loved each other and stuck together through every kind of chaos. We laughed and joked a lot. Toni and I talked and complained a mile a minute through most of her hour and a half. Dan and I talked about more serious things. They said I kept them all from killing each other.

We often talked about Lola as it was Lola who got us together. Toni said she'd had an out-of-body experience while getting a facial from Lola. Those waves and the music lifted her right out of her body, and she was flying over the ocean before she knew it. While completely covered with steaming hot towels, she had also had visions of being stabbed. Lola could make her clients feel that the strangest things were entirely possible.

Just before Lola left for India, she told me she would write a letter to all her clients recommending me for facials. Later I found out she had given her clientele to her ex-husband's wife; the letter had never been written. I also discovered she had promised many people her clientele for $1,000. I was furious. I felt betrayed.

She returned home from India a month after she had left. India didn't suit her. It was too harsh. She was disillusioned.

When she called me, I asked her about our agreement and she apologized, saying she had needed the money and asked me not to be mad, that things had a way of working out. I didn't buy it. I said I thought what she did was dishonest and lacked integrity. She cried on the phone.

The following Sunday Jan called to tell me Lola had killed herself. I didn't think I was responsible, but I felt awful. I wished I had been more kind or forgiving.

Her suicide note said she had died laughing.

Although she didn't give me her facial clients, those she recommended for massage: the woman who wrecked her Rolls Royce, and Toni and Dan were enough. This incident helped me realize that life, the great rectifier, will give me what I need. I believe Lola knew this too.

16

Stars

My clients became more and more star-studded. My phone would ring, and it might be someone I had seen in the movies the night before or on television. Sometimes they were people whose names I'd never heard, but when they opened the door I knew them at once. Because I was dyslexic and didn't read magazines, I would not know them until I saw their faces. Sometimes I would arrive at their gate and be met by a limo that would drive me down the mile-long driveway to the house, where the butler would meet me. I entered these houses as though I were entering a museum: nothing out of place, everything polished and perfect.

The lives of these clients could not have been more unlike mine. In a single day I might massage a woman going to a party with the queen of England that night; then take a hot tub with, then massage a woman married to the president of some oil company; then pound a few inches off the hips of someone going to the Academy Awards in a few hours. These women knew what they thought and they told you so. They knew what they wanted and they went for it. Who was I? What did I want?

After the massage I would go home to my house and listen to the roar of motorcycles ten feet from my window. Because I had no real life of my own I began to glory in the lives of my clients. These wealthy, famous people wanted me, and I lived for that. It was not unusual for them to give me $300 as a tip for a single massage. They would send their jets for me when they were off on location and give me front row tickets to their plays. I wanted so much to be like them.

I absorbed the essence of my clients through my hands. They entered my veins and washed through me. I stole their gestures, their personalities and I carried them with me for hours after a massage.

At times I would catch sight of myself and the life that had absorbed me. I likened myself to a piece of driftwood rushing downstream. I didn't know if I was being polished against the rocks or broken to bits. Sometimes we never know until we enter calm waters and survey what is left.

The lives of my clients reminded me of my childhood dream to be a singer. My parents were passionate about music—classical music. My father was president and my mother was secretary of the community concert series in our town. During the concert season, we had famous violinists, pianists and singers at our home. The pianists would come to practice on our large Grand piano, and others would come to breakfast.

I was not allowed to go to the concerts when I was young. I could not hold still that long. My mother would dress up in wonderful dresses and high heels and go with Dad, leaving me with a sitter. I thought Mom was the most beautiful person in the whole world.

My father was a pianist, but he was never famous like the people who came to our house. When I was young, I vowed to become a famous singer for my father. But as my voice matured, it became apparent I didn't have a classical voice. I loved to sing the blues. When I heard the blues, I thought I heard my soul. But the blues were not allowed in our house, not even on my radio in my own room.

I sang in nightclubs from time to time, but I was frightened of the attention I received and stopped. I stopped singing completely except in the shower when no one else was in the house or in the car on long drives. So I didn't become a singer. My dreams got buried and I lost my way. It was torture to be massaging people who were living out my dreams when I was not using my voice, not even to speak my mind. This went on for years, using these people for my identity because I had no true identity of my own. I couldn't be a star, but I could massage a star. I couldn't be a singer, but I could massage a singer. At least I could look into that world and imagine what it was like. I could touch it.

I felt like Sleeping Beauty surrounded by a thicket, silent as stone.

17

The Countess

ONE OF MY STARS gave my name to a countess and her husband when they were "doing" L.A. one summer. He was a gangster from New Jersey and had leased a villa in Beverly Hills. They flew people in from all over the world to help them find "something to do out there in the "woods", and I massaged them all. The countess was used to life in the cultural centers of Europe, and she did not like L.A.

The gangster was very intrigued with Hitler and studied his methods as if in training for some dark position. He had been involved with governments and knew all about tortures used in Cuba, Vietnam and Korea. He had seen so much violence done to the human body that there were parts of him I couldn't touch. He would say, "We'll skip that part," and a shudder would go off through his muscles as a memory detonated deep inside his nervous system.

The countess was the gangster's whole life. She was a woman who could take the mind of the most tormented man and give him fresh, more immediate things to worry about. For example, she had a habit of disappearing. She kept the gangster chasing her around the world. I heard him on the phone one day after she had disappeared during the night. He paced back and forth across his room making frantic telephone calls to Vienna, Madrid, Paris or Hong Kong. She was a woman made for a man with a secret police and army at his disposal. She knew just what to do with a man like that. She did not take pity on him. She asked for what she wanted and got it. I worshipped her.

She had left heads of state and crown princes waiting to marry her at the altar, with newspapermen smiling at the door chewing on their pencils. I married a man because he had cried when I said, "No."

"How could you do that?" I asked of one such incident. She, of course, thought it was their fault. "They did not have a sense of humor," she said. "They never would have understood me."

She was quite right. No one but the gangster could ever have understood her torment, her rage, her infidelities, and her need to escape at a moment's notice. She needed to have someone track her down and bring her back to safety from the madness that drove her. "If he loves me, he will find me and forgive me," her actions seemed to say.

I believe it was this chase that tied them together. Because there were no more wars to fight or no court that would try him for his crimes against humanity she kept him vibrant and passionate and at the same time miserable over her escapes—which soothed his guilt. By tracking her down no matter where she went, he proved himself and his love over and over again. Through these acts of devotion, intelligence and ability to forgive her anything, her admiration for him stayed alive, which is its own kind of love.

Other men had too much pride for such games. Not the gangster. Not the man who had done something secret in three wars. No, he had no pride. Or at least it wasn't based on something as insignificant as hurt feelings.

The gangster was a master of games of all sorts. I used to play backgammon with him while waiting for the countess to finish her bath or while he was waiting for phone calls from his underground network after she had disappeared. I have never been beaten so quickly every single time. I accused him of having loaded dice and brought my own once. It made no difference.

The countess loved astrology, and once she did my chart. She was surprised I was a Scorpio. She said, "Scorpio's are wild, intense people. What happened to you?" I told her life had worn me down.

She said that it was only a phase, and I would be deliciously horrid again. When her husband chided her about her belief in the stars she would say, "Go read something gruesome about Hitler."

The last time I saw the gangster, he was in despair over another of her disappearances. No army, guard or secret police could protect him from the devastation her leaving caused him. He could not find her anywhere. She finally sent him a note from a European hospital, and he rushed to her side. I heard he never left the hospital until, months later, she died of some stomach ailment.

He never called for a massage again. He never really liked them. He wasn't at home in his body.

I have thought so much about these two as their lives were inexorably woven into mine. Through loving and accepting the gangster, I healed the gangster in me. I have taken my own atrocities —leaving my son, betraying a lover, leaving the convent with the fisherman, breaking the heart of my mother, not remembering the names of God—and made peace with them.

Or perhaps it was the countess who healed them. She would have looked at my problems and flicked them away with a gesture becoming a queen and say, "You are a Scorpio. What can you expect from yourself? You were meant to break hearts. Break more. You have done nothing wrong. Forget it."

I have often wondered what the countess would say if she knew I used her voice, her haughtiness, and the memory of her gestures to exonerate my sins. I know that compared to the sins of the gangster and countess, my sins seemed insignificant. She would probably have a good laugh.

My friend Katherine went to a party one night at the gangster's villa after the countess had died. She told me he had made a shrine of her bedroom.

18

The Lamb

FREQUENTLY I EXCHANGED massage with another masseuse named Kate. During one of these treatments she said she was going on vacation and asked if I would massage some of her clients while she was away. I agreed, and late one Sunday afternoon, I got a call from one of the men to whom she had given my name.

He was a handsome, twenty-nine year old president of something. His home was a mansion overlooking all of Beverly Hills and beyond. He had a manner of speaking that let me know he was used to having his way.

He was draped with a towel and I was massaging the knots in his neck when he told me what marvelous hands I had. This was not an unusual comment, but his tone of voice had changed. I recognized that voice. I had grown ears like microphones listening for that voice. It was the tone of Vaseline, of a person oiling his way into places he didn't belong. When I heard that voice my adrenaline kicked in.

To calm myself I talked about health. I quizzed him about his eating habits and told him clinically about his knots. He swore that he was in the best of health, that it was his work that made him tense.

When I got down to his legs, I knew what was coming; he began to beg me to touch him. "Touch me, touch me, touch me."

We were alone in that large house. No one would have heard my scream. I kept telling him, "I don't do that kind of massage," all the time smiling, giving him my best work. I didn't dare make him mad. I was upset, but I couldn't show my anger. I kept "effleuraging", "petresaging" and kneading. I think I began to hum. It was like saying "Blah, blah, blah" when I was a child unable to cope with what I was hearing. I became that child again.

When the massage was over, I packed up my table without looking at him while he walked across the room to get his robe. He handed me my money, and I left. I cried all the way home in the car. Safe in my house I called a friend and told her what had happened. She said, "Why didn't you tell him to get the hell off your table?" I didn't know. I hadn't thought of it. Why couldn't I protect myself?

I confronted Kate about this man when she returned. She said, "I told him I didn't think you would go for it. In fact I made him promise to be good."

"What do you mean? Do you do sexual massage?" I asked astounded.

"Well, only when I want to," she replied. "It's very profitable."

I was shocked. I felt naive, provincial, stupid and curious all at the same time.

Why did I take everyone else's side against my own? Could I be all things to all people because I was no one in particular? Asking myself these questions and staying with the feelings, I finally got the answer. I had been six years old. I went across the street to play with my friend Bobby. Bobby wasn't home, but his uncle was. His uncle invited me in and took me upstairs to his bedroom. He laid me down on the bed. He said we would play a kissing game. He promised me a quarter a kiss for every place he kissed me. He kissed my neck, and then he took off my clothes. Each time, before he kissed me, he asked, "Can I kiss you here?" And in my memory I heard a little, scared voice say, "Yes." I didn't know I could say, "No" to an adult.

Remembering that time, I entered the body of myself as a child. I swallowed my "no" and rationalized that I was going to get a quarter, and as I did so, I split my mind off from my experience; I disassociated. I betrayed myself with my own voice.

I couldn't tell my parents. I'd said yes to everything. When Bobby's uncle was through with me I wasn't even sure what had happened. The only thing I knew for sure was that he hadn't given me a single quarter, and I had been too shy to remind him.

After remembering the incident with Bobby's uncle, I was flooded with other memories, memories with names, dates and faces that before had only been screams or nightmares. I felt as if my brain was a large computer sorting through it's files, flipping through its folds, muttering, "I know it's in here somewhere next to 'light,' no, 'lever,' no, 'lamb'—that's it." And lamb went with uncle, but not Bobby's uncle. Lamb went with my own uncle, Uncle Bill.

I never liked Uncle Bill or his wife, Myrtle. Bill always had tobacco juice running down his chin. He talked so slowly I would forget what he was saying. Myrtle talked fast, like the chickens. Even though Bill and Myrtle had chosen different styles of talking, both had taken on the sounds of the barnyard: caws, cackles and grunts.

Uncle Bill and Aunt Myrtle's farm always had kittens and puppies, hens and warm eggs in the hen house, and this particular Saturday there were lambs. I was shown the lambs and allowed to pet one of them. It was the softest thing I had ever touched. Then Uncle Bill told me to go away, and the lamb was led to the barn. When I tried to follow Uncle Bill and my father, I was told to leave, which made me want to stay all the more.

Uncle Bill tied a rope around the hind feet of the lamb and, with a pulley pulled it, upside down, into the air. The lamb bleated in terror and pain. I looked on in horror, then began screaming and begging them to stop, to let it down, and later, to hurry and put it out of its misery. I could feel the lamb's pain enter me. It was as if I was hanging there. Finally, my father demanded that I leave. I remember listening to the lamb bleating from the garden where I was told to stay. I could not stop crying.

Later I crept back to the barn and saw the lamb hanging with its throat cut and no skin. I knew my father and uncle had done that. I stared at the bloody body. I was filled with horror and sickness, trying to make sense of it. I dreamed of the lamb, imagining what its death must have been like. I imagined being tied upside down, my throat being cut, skin torn off, helpless.

Was this why I wanted to comfort the world with my touch? Was I trying to create a world of softness that I could live in?

The shock of remembering Bobby's uncle and the memory of the lamb cracked the wall that had been protecting me from my past. And as all my ghosts oozed out of the cracks, my emotions exploded out of me like a volcano, exposing all I wanted to keep hidden and burying all my defenses.

19

The Shadow Side

AFTER MY EXPERIENCE with Kate's client, and her response, the part of me that had been hiding behind layers of denial, temporary roles, New Age philosophies, prayers, yoga and abstinence came out and demanded its time and its voice. I knew I was in trouble the day a new client came to me. He was a scriptwriter who reminded me of Napoleon. When he lay on my table on his stomach and I massaged his scalp he stroked my hips, and I didn't move away. After several weeks he said, "You have given me more pleasure than any one person in my whole life."

I found I wore less and less when Napoleon came. Thin skirts replaced my thick, white trousers. My sexless white blouses were exchanged for tank tops or leotards. But the day I would have allowed him to take me, he was preoccupied with his movie. Something about the perception of his movie had changed for him. At one time he thought his script was a grand idea. Then on the day I wore no bra or panties under my thin dress, on that day he saw his movie for the shallow, idiotic, boyish and trivial thing it was, and it took all the fire and confidence out of him, and I was spared. Though he came back for massage, the spell was broken, and my attraction to him died.

Next there was the businessman who came to my house to have privacy from his wife. It turned out that his wife and he had never been sexually compatible, even with four children, he said. He was confident of his good looks, though he did not appeal to me. I do not like pretty men. Give me someone with a scar or someone who has had his heart torn out; someone who is lost or broken.

When I looked at this man, I saw the flabbiness of his character, and I hated him. He had the best of life too easily. He was a tree who had all the room it needed to grow straight and tall, the right amount of water, rich soil and sunlight. He had become proud of his thick branches and was stingy and vain.

And I was scared. My need for money, love and approval was struggling with my image of the "good girl." Two sides were warring within me, wanting to live a life of sex with strangers, wanting to tell this man how much I despised him, but fighting against the part of me wanting to take him in my mouth and be his darling. I wanted to shock him, tie his hands behind his back and tease every one of his pressure points. I wanted to arouse him until he came violently with a single kiss; I wanted to dive into the riptide that was pulling me under and down.

The day he called to say he was coming over, not for massage but just to see me, I wrote him a note and left it outside on my door. It read, "I don't want you for a friend, and I don't want you for a client. I don't want you to call me. I never want to see you again." Then I went to the beach and cried and walked Hoover until I knew the man had come and gone.

After that there was an actor who had been flirting with me for a year. He called from New York one day and asked if I would come to work on him before his play. I was flattered. He sent me plane fare, and when I arrived, he met my plane. He even took me to meet his parents. The play was a huge success, and I had a seat in the front row. He was attentive at the party afterward and introduced me to everyone.

After making love with him all night and a day, I massaged him with my hair and my thighs and my breasts. And as I sank deeper into this land filled with taboo, I realized that my fascination with sexual power and the thrill of the forbidden were stronger than my will to resist.

The confusion caused by having sex with a client—one I knew would never be my boyfriend or my husband—and my inability to stop it were a horror. It was as if the meaning of my life was just out of reach, and if I went just a little deeper into the unknown, I would find out what that meaning was. I judged myself horribly, the pain of which made me rationalize this behavior. "This was not a client," I told myself. "He was my client, then he was my lover, then massage and sex got confused. They were happening at the same time. That was not the same thing as being a whore, not the same thing at all." My guilt forced me to try to make my relationship with this actor more than it was, and we never saw each other again.

And finally there was Richard. Richard, the same name as my father. Richard, the same age as my father. Richard, who looked just like my father.

Richard's wife had heard about me and asked me to come massage them both. I massaged her first. Then he came bouncing in entirely naked. He hardly spoke during the first massage.

During the second massage, his wife was being interviewed by a woman's magazine in the living room while I massaged Richard in the bedroom. He called me his little philosopher, his little poetess. I told him he had a tummy in order to give him some humility. He said his sexpot wife put all her energy into her career, and he couldn't even get laid. He was so adorable and honest that my heart went out to him, and I couldn't help reaching down and patting his cock. He gave me $400 for the massage, though I charged only $75.

A month had gone by when Richard's houseboy called and said Richard wanted a massage. It would only be him as his wife was out of town. At the last minute I decided not to go. Then Richard called me from a health spa a few hours from L.A. and asked me to come there; I gave in.

Richard had instructed me to wait outside the entrance to the spa. It had taken me two hours to drive there. I parked, got some coffee and drank it in the car while watching for Richard in the rearview mirror. Glamorous people walked by talking about glamorous things. Dressed-to-the-teeth women got out of Mercedes and Stingrays, Porches and Rolls', and I became more and more insecure. I could hear the voices in my head begin to sneer. After forty-five minutes waiting in the red zone, I left a message that I had gone home. I had driven two hours and waited forty-five minutes to be a whore to a man who never showed up.

Part of me was thanking God as I drove away, and another was shaking with anger. I became hysterical in the car, driving down the freeway at seventy miles per hour. I was shocked when I began to scream, "Daddy, daddy, daddy."

I arrived home and went straight to the bathtub. I was going to lock myself in and not answer the door. I was going to call the six people coming to dinner that night and cancel. I was going to sit and demand that God change my life before I went on with it another step.

But the tide would not let go of me. The phone kept ringing. I knew it was Richard. Finally I answered it.

He said, "Why did you leave?"

I said, "How could you treat me this way?"

He said, "Don't be mad. I told you I might be late. I couldn't get away. I was desperate to get away. I was so anxious at lunch that my family said I seemed preoccupied. I was looking forward to seeing you, and I am so sorry this happened. Please come back. You can spend the night."

"No."

"I will send my plane."

"Not tonight, I'm too upset."

"Well, tomorrow. I'll send my plane tomorrow."

I said I would see how I felt the next morning.

The next morning he called. He was coming to L.A., and I should come to his house at six. We would then fly to the spa.

When I arrived at Richard's house, all the usually locked doors were open. The pool was lit. As soon as he saw me, he raced over and began kissing me, unzipping me, and pushing me toward the bedroom. I didn't expect this to happen until after eating and talking and flying and looking and flirting and kissing and touching—

gentle touching. I did not expect this, not like this. No, no, not like this.

But I was not this man's woman; I was there for a purpose. We had agreed not to name it. We had agreed to put a mask on it. And all the while I remembered Kate saying, "It takes me days to recover. I am exhausted after. Your will is stripped away from you. Nothing is left. All your water is taken, and it comes back alone, in horror, drop by drop."

I thought these things lying on Richard's bed. I was not in my body. I was somewhere else watching, waiting for it to be over—until I got aroused myself and it brought me back, and I couldn't escape. I was there wanting, wanting. I couldn't stop wanting. Desire was pulling me into this man's arms, my father's arms, my rapist's arms, my molester's arms. And the guilt for loving it was unbearable.

How does a person live when conquered by an enemy? A body, mind and soul shackled by the shadow side—how does it survive? Words of war come to mind: internment, captivity, broken, demoralized, prisoner of war, dungeons, chains, slaughter, casualty, the dead, the fallen, the lost-in-action, numbered with the dead, massacred, war-torn. A person occupied by the enemy waits, listens and stays alive by not thinking too much, by barely breathing.

The first night I was with Richard, after sex and after dinner, we drove to the airport where we boarded his plane. An army of people were waiting for him. He told me, "Just smile and let them think what they want." Once in the air his steward brought us coffee and kiwi, and I looked out the window at all the bright lights.

The experience with him that night shook me to my core. I went places with him that rocked every idea I had of good and evil, right or holy. All those concepts were ground to sand, then melted. By the time Richard slept, my body was numb. I was thinking I might cry, but I didn't. My feelings were indistinguishable. I was emptiness itself.

That night I had a dream. Someone was making love to me. In the dream I opened my eyes and found it was my son. I woke up. It was as though my inner child was coming with a message. I did not understand. I felt sick.

At 9:15 A.M. as I was getting ready for the steward to pick me up from the spa in San Diego and take me back home to L.A., Richard followed me around showing me a birthday card he had picked out for his granddaughter and a new brochure for one of his stores. At the car he said he would call me when he got back to L.A., and then he handed me an envelope.

In the plane the bright sun made everything flat. The glittering lights of the city were burned out. I didn't look inside the envelope until I reached my car. Inside were ten hundred-dollar bills. I sat looking at them, wondering who I was. All the way home and for many days after, I had a compulsion to buy ridiculous things I didn't need. I wanted to get rid of that money.

I knew I could not be Richard's mistress. I was not made to be a mistress. I would have fallen in love with him, and it would have been the end of me. I could picture myself following him around the world, sitting in suites in expensive hotels, waiting and crying. I would have had to be a secret. I knew I couldn't bear it no matter how much money Richard showered on me.

Then a miracle occurred. My son came to live with me. After thirteen long years living apart, except for summers, he finally came to live with me. I did not want to be a mistress. I wanted to be a mother.

When my son came to live with me, he was sixteen. It was 1985. He moved in with me because I lived in a school district that had a highly rated swim coach who said he could get Russell on a college swim team. Phil wanted Russell to have that experience.

When our living together became permanent, Russell's anger at me for leaving him began to emerge. He wouldn't talk to me.

He would come home from school, go into his room and shut the door, coming out only for meals. He wouldn't tell me anything about his life, what he felt, what he was doing, what he wanted— nothing.

I sat in the living room hoping for a glimpse of him. To find out how he was doing, I eavesdropped when he called his father. My anxiety was almost uncontainable. I waited and waited—taking him to swim meets, praying while I cooked that the food would not burn, (I wasn't at all domestic), shopping for his favorite foods: chicken without bones, pineapple in chunks with small curd cottage cheese, processed whole wheat bread, spaghetti with canned sauce, no onions, oatmeal or cream of wheat with raisins and honey.

He would not celebrate Christian holidays, so we celebrated Jewish ones. Over Easter we ate peanut butter sandwiches on the beach and watched the surfers at Malibu Point while Hoover chased seagulls.

When Russell came to live with me, all my sixteen-year-old issues were coming to the surface. We were both emotionally sixteen at the same time; only I was in a thirty-nine-year-old body. But the mother in me was also longing to be born.

I believe it was through daily rituals that Russell began to trust me. It was small things at first: buying small curd cottage cheese, giving him a shoulder massage just before going to bed, watching M*A*S*H together on TV on a regular basis and picking him up at swimming practice on time. All these constant activities made it possible for him to open up and begin talking to me again. We began to heal the things that could be healed.

At the end of Russell's senior year of high school, his swim team won the All City Championship. Mom, Phil and I went and yelled our heads off . There was a banquet to celebrate. Russell had been elected captain of the swim team that year and gave a speech at the banquet. He was eloquent. In the speech he thanked the swim team, and especially me, for making it the best year of his life. I could have died right then and felt my life was complete. After graduation Russell went to college in a town nearby and we saw each there often.

Even though I had stopped being Richard's mistress and my son had come to live with me, my personal journey into darkness continued. Something was trying to come up; like a bubble of air deep in a lake, like a sliver in the flesh, something did not belong in me, and it was coming to the surface.

After Richard, all my attempts to find love ended in disaster. I could not look directly at a man. I stopped massaging for a while and worked as a secretary in an all girls' school. Then temptation came from women who said they wanted to have affairs with me. It was as if temptation came to me under the door, through the vents, through songs, through movies, plays and dreams.

And one day after lunch, driving down a street in Pasadena, my father said, "I wonder how we have lived all these years without making love? Do you ever think crazy things like that? I love you so much, much more than just a daughter. You are the love of my life."

I became numb when he told me this. I went into a survival mode, which was very familiar. All my feelings shut down as though a switch had been thrown. I could barely breathe. A smile appeared on my face. Three days later I hesitatingly asked a friend, "Is that a strange thing to say to a daughter?"

Nine months later when I told my father on the phone that I was seeing an old high school boyfriend who had found me after twenty-two years, he said drunkenly, "Does this mean I have lost you for good?" And he sobbed as if his heart would break.

A month later I wrote my father a letter. In it I told him these statements had made so much clear to me. I told him I always knew he had loved me inappropriately.

He wrote back that he had never said those things, that he had burned my letter, and that I should not ever mention it again. He couldn't imagine what I was talking about.

With each word of denial, I felt a bomb exploding. Shrapnel landed in huge chunks around me. Finally I opened my eyes, and the sun was gone and I did not know how to be a safe container for my feelings.

In time I began to understand why I never went to see my father, why I never thought of him, why he hardly existed in my life. In order to be close to him, I would have to tell him the truth about himself, and somewhere, long ago, we had agreed to lie. An unspoken message had been conveyed that his wanting me as a lover would never be acknowledged or admitted. It could be expressed through touch, lewd jokes, and glances, but we would never say the words. If it were put into words, the meaning would be known, and no one, not Dad or Mom or me could bear it.

When I accepted the truth about my father, other memories seeped back. I remembered that when I was a teenager he would get me drunk and come onto me as though I were a lover. Getting drunk allowed him to cross the line of taboos, and though I was disgusted I couldn't tell him. I protected him from knowing what he was doing. I protected him at the expense of protecting myself. I had been trained well by both my mother and my father not to expose them or even let them know what they were doing. It was as if I had been forced to become blind. And when he hugged me and touched my breasts, I never said a word. Not one.

And when I had my son—dear heart of my heart—I was terrified to touch him. His love reached in so deep. The bright ray of his love illuminated all my darkness. Russell's helplessness tormented me because it reminded me of my own. What was hidden in me could not be expressed. There were no words. I was never allowed to name my suffering. I could only run away from what I loved the most for fear of hurting him.

So some wise part of me had left him with his father until I got sober and knew what I was doing. Some good part of me or some saint I had prayed to had mercy on us both.

20

Memories Emerging

As I became accustomed to living with the feelings these memories produced in me, I began to realize how I had shut myself away. I had created a world I could live in. I had created a safe, protected room and lived in it. I comforted everyone who came to me as though they were my own self, the lamb, the victims of the world. Making friends with my rage, which I had never expressed, and with all the feelings of betrayal and loss, I began to attract women clients who had been through similar experiences. Soon after my experience with Richard, I massaged Carla. We had been friends for a long time, but I had never massaged her. To begin, she lay on her stomach, and I rocked her gently back and forth a hundred times or more. As I rocked her, the table creaked in rhythm like waves. As I rocked her, I remembered rocking my son, and myself, hearing lullabies, swinging, and leaves swaying.

Perhaps our friendship allowed us to move into a very deep state. I stood at her head, thumbs on each side of her spine. As I leaned forward they slid down her back. I hovered over the tension in her shoulders, her freeway, coffee, rush-filled shoulders. Her upper back was locked and stiff, holding in, holding back, but when I reached her buttocks I knew I'd found her holding flesh. She was so sore in her hips, I could barely touch her. Places that sore hold trauma.

As I massaged my friend's hips, she told me a story. She remembered it there on my table. "Remember" is not the right word because it had never been forgotten. No, she really let the story come out.

She had been six years old, playing in a barn, when a gang of older boys came in and raped her. She didn't tell a soul. For the next several years they hounded her, making her do it again and again. When she finally said "No, no more," the boys threatened her and then told everyone in the small, country town what she had done, that she had let them do it.

My friend told me that when she was in the second grade, she was afraid to look at anyone. They all knew what had happened, what she had done. When her father found out about the boys in the barn, he beat her. When her grandfather heard, he took advantage of the situation by molesting her himself, then warned her, "If you tell, I'll spank you."

Carla had been hanging her head in shame ever since, but she had forgotten why until the day I massaged her hips. Soon after that the rage came, and a very good therapist helped her remove those sick people she had been carrying within her for so long.

Though I never identified her, I carried Carla's story to a client whose name was Barbara. I often use stories to help a client open up. Every story is a teaching. I was massaging Barbara's chest, softening the muscles around the cavity where her lungs empty and fill, empty and fill.

Barbara had asked me to give her an example of how the body stores memories so I told her about Carla.

During the story, Barbara began to sob.

"What's wrong?" I asked.

Barbara had a daughter, Martina. At three-years-old she went to a day care center. One day several boys entered the girls' bathroom. She was there, alone. They threw her to the floor, and while they held her arms down and her legs apart they raped her with the sticks and rocks they carried. They pulled the sticks in and out of her tiny vagina and when they were done, the boys walked away, leaving her there, all alone.

Martina didn't tell the teacher. Perhaps at three she didn't have language for what had happened. Perhaps she was ashamed. No one knew until her bath that night when her daddy lowered her into the warm water and she screamed in pain. Blood and pus were still visible. They rushed her to an emergency room where a doctor put her three-year-old feet in stirrups and, under the bright light, cleaned rocks and fragments of wood and dirt out of her.

Barbara and her husband called the school and arranged to meet with the principal and the boys' parents. One family never showed up; the second couple got in a fight in the office, and the father said it must have been Martina's fault. The third couple said it couldn't have been their son.

Four years later when Martina entered regular school, she still sucked her thumb incessantly. She didn't pay attention, and she didn't participate. She had a rash around her mouth from nervously licking it. The teacher was frustrated and told Barbara and her husband that Martina needed a psychologist.

"Did you tell the psychologist about her being raped?" I asked Barbara.

"No, I have not thought about it for a long time," she said. "The story you told me brought it all back. How could I have forgotten?"

I was massaging Barbara's feet. We were both crying. I had known this family for five years. Each member was precious to me. I was also crying because I know how easy it is to forget. The mind wants to forget. After making breakfast a thousand times, going on vacations, getting dressed, doing laundry, taking the dogs to the vet, getting through the in-laws' visits, celebrating holidays, buying furniture, coping with deaths, going to movies, watching wars, having financial problems, the mind covers up painful memories. We rage more and drink too much and can't concentrate as well, but we excuse it all by thinking, "That's what happens with age." We plaster over the memory of our baby girl lying on a bathroom floor being brutally raped. Instead of grieving we run marathons and shop more until that memory is sealed in solid iron.

The next day Barbara told her daughter's therapist. He kept repeating during their conversation, "I can't tell you how important this is. I can't tell you how important this is. I can't tell you how important this is. People commit murder later in life because of things like this they have never talked about."

I called Carla, whose story I had told, to let her know a little girl was being helped because she had shared her story. "Don't be ashamed to tell your story," I told her. She said she would tell it on the street corner and sing it on the radio. Carla was forty-five before she remembered her own sexual abuse. So much of her life might have been different had her mother helped her deal with what had happened. When Carla finally told her mother, she told Carla of her own incest and how helpless she had felt. When Carla asked why she hadn't told her before, her mother said, "You don't talk about such things."

And what happened to the boys? Where did they learn to hate women so young? Where are they now? Will they ever learn to respect their own softness or nurture a female body? Will they have baby girls of their own?

21

Creating a Cocoon

FOR WEEKS I grieved about Martina. Whenever I thought of her father lowering her into the warm bath, or her little feet in stirrups under the bright lights at the hospital, I fell apart. These images were unbearable to me. After hearing this story, I went home and went to bed. I took all that pain, both hers and mine and felt the full power of it in my body. I held myself in that pain as though I were a hurt child. And I told myself, "I will not leave myself. I will not get up for anyone, until I feel like it."

Several days later, I was driving down Pacific Coast Highway when I felt all the blood drain from my face. My body felt as though I were waking up from a deep sleep. I remembered when I was sixteen and became pregnant by a boy I deeply loved. My parents nearly killed me. They put me in a hot bath for many hours and gave me pills my father got from a prostitute that was supposed to produce miscarriage. When that failed, they forced me to drink a pint of gin, which was supposed to make me sick and cause the miscarriage. It didn't. I got alcohol poisoning instead. Then they drove me to Tijuana to an abortionist who tied me to a table. There was no anesthetic.

After that my mother watched for my periods like a hawk.

I paid dearly for my passion at the hands of my parents, but the offense that hardened me was of my own doing. The offense to my own life that chained me, like Prometheus to the rock was committed months later after the abortion. My mother suspected I had seen my lover again, and she threatened me, "I will not go through another abortion with you. If you haven't started your period by tomorrow, I will put you into a foster home."

That night I went to bed with a snakebite kit and a Kotex pad. Mother would not send me away from my home, my school, and the boy I loved. She did not know how scared I was. I thought I might be pregnant again. But I would not give into her again. I would not be vulnerable again.

I thought these things while getting into bed. Taking out the blade, I still didn't believe I would do it. Squeezing my hand, I made the blood rush down to the tips of my fingers. I still didn't believe I was capable of going through with it until some sort of trance came over me. The power to have my way went deep within me and connected with a source that had been there all the time. I just had to find it. It is a power that can be found only by blocking out the warning signals of fear that listens to nothing that sounds like a whimper. This power has no pity, especially for itself. It is a power that abolishes the fear of God. It is hubris, pure and simple—the one sin the gods will not forgive.

I cut every one of my fingers and squeezed the blood out drop by drop onto the pad until the white cotton was stained bright red. I placed it between my legs and wore it into the right shape and showed it to my mother the next morning.

The last time there was a chance of being brought back to vulnerability and softness was a few days later. I was washing dishes with my mother, and she saw my hands. She picked up one hand and looked deeply into my eyes. There was horror in her eyes. She didn't understand; the meaning of what she was seeing would not come to her. I can't imagine she thought I cut myself like that by accident. She let go of my hand and walked away not saying a word. She let go of my hand, and I was lost.

This power led me to having illicit affairs, drinking, stealing, doing drugs, dealing drugs, running red lights, sneaking out of places I belonged and into places I didn't. I didn't feel the consequences, didn't know there were consequences until I lost my son, and then, no matter what I did or where I put myself, the pain would not go away.

My mother eventually became exhausted from policing me and sent me to a foster home anyway. It wasn't so bad during the day. My life was filled with being in a new high school and finding my way through the maze of new faces. I was caught up in being sixteen, mastering my hair, my walk, and my smile. It was here I learned to walk with my breath. When I walked to school, I walked slow, one breath for one step. I found this had a hypnotizing effect on me.

At night when everyone in my new home was peacefully asleep, I could not hold still in bed. I was so enraged I couldn't sleep. I just could not forget the abortion and the doctor telling me, "Don't move or the knife could slip, and you could bleed to death." I missed my boyfriend, Doug. My parents had the court issue an order making it illegal for him to see me until I was eighteen. I missed my cat, who had slept next to me, purring, for years. When my fury at being removed from my home and all that I loved overwhelmed me, I would creep out of bed and walk up and down the stairs, one breath per step.

One night the thoughts in my head would not stop. My mind kept screaming the names of my boyfriend, my cat, and my horse. "Doug, Star, Mittens, Star. Doug, Mittens, Star. Doug, Mittens, Star." I would try to hold their images like a hug, as if naming them would bring them to me. But naming them only made their absence more real, and before I knew it, I was rushing over the edge, out of the lines, farther and farther out. I didn't think I could make it to the next moment if there wasn't someone to hold me, something to comfort me, something familiar. I began to say, "Wall, floor, ceiling, walking, carpet, stairs," pacing the stairwell naming the things I could recognize, trying desperately to have something make sense, make my mind safe.

I could feel the hysteria swelling in me, growing bigger and bigger inside me. I couldn't scream and wake the strangers I now lived with. How could I explain my scream to strangers? What would strangers do if my own parents, who were supposed to love me, who said they loved me, let me go, kicked me out? If they had done this to me, what would strangers do? I couldn't scream; I couldn't make a sound. I couldn't risk finding out what strangers would do. I could only open my mouth and pretend to scream. I could only scream in a whisper, "Wall, ceiling, carpet, stairs, wall, ceiling, carpet, stairs."

The pain in my chest became bigger than me and there was no way for me to control it, not by myself, not alone. Someone needed to be there, but there was no one, only strangers. And when it got too big to contain, I exploded. I flew apart into hundreds of pieces right there on the stairs. No one ever knew I exploded that night, but I did. I exploded into so many pieces I knew I would never be me again.

Exhausted, I went to bed.

I was amazed the next morning when Charlie Mae, the foster mother, recognized me. She made me breakfast and sent me off to school as if I was the same person I had been the day before. But I knew I wasn't. I walked slower than ever to school that day naming the things I saw, whispering, "Flowers, lawn, house, red roof, doorway, tree."

As I walked, I heard someone inside me ask for comfort, and very soon I was given a Marlboro. And I asked for comfort again, and the comforter came back Jack Daniel. And something rose out of me like a big black bird and flew through the land crying for oblivion. And all the dark things in the world heard and descended into me, feeding me, anesthetizing me, comforting me in my cocoon of emptiness, my cocoon of hardness.

And when anyone came along to love me, a friend, a lover, my son, I was terrified to open and I left.

22

Breakdown

STANDING IN THE KITCHEN wanting tea, I would stare at the faucet and not remember how to get hot water, the cup and the tea bag together. The more I tried to push my mind to recall this magic, the more anxious and fearful I would get until I was hysterical. It was 1989. I was forty-one, not sixteen. Or was I? I was bedeviled with fragments of thoughts and images that couldn't come together. I was falling into unconnected pieces.

I would look at Hoover, whom I knew needed a walk. Then I would remember I hadn't eaten that day, and I would start bath-water. I would walk down the hall to the kitchen to get something to eat with one leg in a pair of jeans, the other bare for my bath and not be able to decide which should be done first or how to do it if I made a decision. I would end up pounding on my bed, screaming until I passed out from pure exhaustion, awaking the next day, every vertebra out of place. I screamed out the misery collected in my guts, veins, lymphatic cesspools, and the glands surrounding the pelvis that had captured my tears for years.

I couldn't hold still. I couldn't let the feelings come up. The clients that came, all with their rage or hunger or incest, began tearing away at the fabric of my cocoon. I emerged raw, without protection. It was my dark night of the soul.

In America we have no guides to explain this form of initiation. We call doctors who put us in hospitals and give us drugs so we won't feel as bad as we truly feel. They hide the Self from the self. When we buy the deceit and have successfully stuffed everything in place once more, the doctors sign our release, and we are free to roam the streets once more, slack-jawed with vacant eyes.

I did not take drugs. If I had, I might never have found my way out of the madness. Nor did I call a doctor. Instead I cried and pounded and ached and talked and wrote and cried and pounded and ached and wrote and ached and cried and pounded and ached and ached and wrote and cried and pounded and wrote for months.

I didn't dare go to the movies or listen to the radio. A strong emotional scene or song could send me into uncontrollable aching and longing that lasted for days. It took months before I had a glimmer of hope that I would ever be well again.

It has been my experience that if we become religious or spiritual without doing our psychological work, we often use the rules of a church or spiritual path or guru in lieu of maturing individually. We live through a set of "ideals" rather than trusting our own experience. This keeps true spiritual experience from being able to reach you.

For me to live authentically—that is, to be true to my own nature—I had to enter my body. I did that by sinking down into my humanity, not trying to "rise above it." To live in a place of soul I had to sink down into all that pain, loneliness, despair, experience and rage and grieve until I burned out all that was false, leaving only my essence. I believe this is the true meaning of alchemy.

During this time, while all this was coming to the surface, I could not bear to see my mother. There are times the people we love just get in the way. They want to spare you the pain of growth. I did not see my mother for almost a year. When we finally got together, she was angry. She said I blamed her for everything. I screamed at her, "You almost killed me." I lost control completely as I told her about the long-reaching effects the abortion and the foster home had had on me.

After our fight I ran from the house and went down to the river. I thought, "She will never speak to me again." But within a few minutes she came to me and threw her arms around me. She said, "I am so sorry I hurt you. Please forgive me."

It was all I'd ever wanted just to have her acknowledge what she had done. I had many friends and clients whose parents had chosen never to speak to them again rather than admit guilt.

My mother said, "Let's take two rocks and throw them in the river. They will represent our past." When I handed her a rock, she said, "That one's not big enough."

When we threw the rocks into the water, we agreed to start over, and we have. The empty place where love of mother should have been was soon filled with love again. We have become friends.

My awareness of the darkness in my life seemed to pull out the darkness in my clients. Everyone who came to me became aware of something that had been blocked. I believe that facing my own demons changed my chemistry and this change worked for others. I believe grieving is a political act. When we have the courage to grieve, we do so for everyone.

23

Sarah

SARAH SOUGHT ME OUT because she had migraines and hoped massage would help. I learned she was obsessed with the homeless and did volunteer work to find ways to feed and house them. She always had a petition to be signed, a cause that needed funds.

I once went with Sarah on her rounds. She knew the names of the people I passed every day; people in front of the post office, sitting on the sidewalk amid a heap of rags and junk they had piled around them like a fort. I always thought of homeless people as mythic creatures or characters out of a Greek drama, some archetype that was coming out of the psyche of America that we had kept under and out of sight as long as we could. Sarah knew them by name.

Usually when Sarah had a migraine, she would call and cancel her massage, but one day the migraine came while she was on my table. Sarah said it felt like there was a monster, lurking in her shoulders, about to climb onto the base of her neck.

I said, "I would like to meet this monster. Can you ask it to talk to me?"

She thought my request was silly, but she agreed to play my game.

I asked the monster, "Who are you, and what do you need?"

The monster replied, "I am the internal wounds, the deformity of Sarah. I want to be seen."

"By whom?" I asked.

"By her parents, the world, everyone."

I said, "I see you and you are enormous. I am very sorry you were so damaged. What do you need to feel better?"

The monster said, "I am unfixable. There is nothing to do. I only want to be seen."

I had to respect that. There are many things that are unfixable by anything we consciously know. Sometimes we need to include and make friends with the parts of ourselves that are unspeakably painful and horrible. I saw clearly why Sarah worked with the homeless; they looked like she felt inside. Their plight was enormously complex, their problems too large to imagine.

24

Katrina

WHEN I BEGIN A MASSAGE, the first things I look for
are the major spots of tension and pain. Then I ask, "What is the
body saying?" The possibilities are endless. Shoulders can say, "Help
me," or "I hate you," or "don't leave me." I have heard them.

I have heard feet say, "You are killing me; I can not go on."
Backs, "It is hopeless." Necks, "Let go, let go." Arms, "Hold me."

Bodies can tell of witches in the pancreas, wolves in the spleen,
and the need to spill your guts. We must listen and believe them.

I feel like a detective, staying open as each new clue presents itself.
It is tempting to say, "Oh, this is why you are the way you are." The
mind loves certainty, wants to know everything immediately, wants to
be healed immediately, but pain is our guide. If we suppress the pain in
our bodies, it will eventually find another way to express itself. It is
telling us something we are unwilling or unable to say out loud, and so
the body says it for us. If the pain could talk, it might say, "Hello, hello.
You aren't saying how much pain you are in. You are smiling when you
really want to hit someone."

Katrina was like that.

Katrina was the daughter of a judge, wife of a famous journalist,
mother of lawyers. She was an executive in a large corporation. I had
never felt such all-over stiffness in my life, except for Mr. Pillsbury,
who was dying of Parkinson's.

Katrina had had a car accident that left her with a whiplash,
which is why she came to me. She reported almost driving into a
pole on the freeway on her way to see me, and that weekend she'd

almost driven off a cliff near Big Sur. I prayed for courage before I asked her, "Why are you trying to kill yourself?"

She was stunned by the question. She said she couldn't relate to the idea. She was very happy with her life. I knew she had everything she wanted and so this might be true.

"That may be," I said bravely, "but there is a part of you that is most definitely trying to kill you, and we'd better have a talk with that part of you."

Katrina was shaken by her near disaster. She would have tried anything.

I said a prayer, "Guide us safely." Then I told her to breathe deeply, then faster and faster. I had learned this technique, called rebirthing, many years before and had seldom used it. It brings up awareness from the unconscious so quickly that most people can't integrate it. Rebirthing opens the psyche by force. But I knew this woman and her grasp on reality. I knew it was life and death.

I heard her breath take over. She was no longer forcing herself to breathe; the breath became a force of its own. It was on the path, taking her back, bulldozing the walls that kept out memories, rushing through overgrown forests, and then a gasp. Ah, she is there. Tears down her cheek, yes, yes, she is there, in the room, in her father's closet the day of his funeral, smelling his jackets, saying, "I won't live without you. I want to die, too."

She had forgotten this vow, this promise sealed by emotion, but her body hadn't. That closet shocked her system. I was shocked watching her.

Her vision was only the beginning. In her father's closet she turned around and said, "I will make earth my home. I will live out my life as it comes to me, no matter what the price."

There were years of integrating to do, pieces of herself to pick up, sort out, forgive. Ultimately she could choose to say good-bye to her father and promise to live with the living.

25

The Tear

JANET CAME TO ME after seeing an article of mine about stories in the body, published in *Women of Power*. She could not believe I had used the word "cunt" in print. She wanted to meet me because of that word. Amazing, our unknown signals reaching out to each other through the maze of media, through the channels of air filled with static and microwaves.

Janet was the youngest child and her father's favorite. At the age of four she was forced by her mother to make her father sign papers admitting him to Camarillo Mental Hospital for depression. He had become intolerable to Janet's mother, and she was convinced that in the hospital he would get proper care.

Janet's mother piled all the children and her father in the car and drove to the hospital without telling anyone where they were going. Once there, her mother told Janet to plead with her father to sign the papers admitting him. Janet was not allowed to cry, nor ask about her father while he was "away." Her mother, who was overworked with six children, would not allow it.

Janet put her pain, her fear, and her love of her father in her back, neck, shoulders, hips, face, legs, and arms. This perfect body, this body on which there was not one ounce of fat or cellulite, was rigid as stone.

Janet told me she had been in partnership with a man for three years. She said that she didn't love him, but she couldn't bear to hurt him by leaving. She couldn't leave her boss either, even though she hated her job. "What would he do without me? Who would answer the phone and pay the bills? Who would support him?"

When I said, "What were the words you wanted to say when you were four standing at the admitting desk at Camarillo? Tell me your story of the silent ride home with your mother, brothers and sisters," Janet held her breath. A tear trickled down her cheek. Not a muscle in her face moved with emotion. Not a gasp of breath escaped her. The tear was the only sign she had heard me.

She never came back for massage. She called months later to say she would come back when she had enough money. I do not believe she lacked money. I think she was afraid of the feelings she now knew were inside her. To relax she would have to experience those feelings, and she just wasn't ready.

26

Mimi

I HAD KNOWN MIMI for years. At forty-five she was an executive in a company that did fundraising for organizations. She came to me for a massage when her regular therapist, with whom she had been doing incest work for years, was away on vacation.

Mimi told me that not long before she came to me, she had been praying on her knees in her bathroom, "Please God, give me the strength to face all that is blocking me from living completely." When she stood up, she lost her balance, hit her shoulder and head on the bathtub, and lost consciousness.

While I massaged her neck, I asked her to blow out the color of the blockage she felt. Her neck was a mass of steel. The color of the block was black, she said. I felt so much resistance in me when I touched her. Her skin was clammy. It felt evil. Not that Mimi was evil, but as though some evil had come into her, perhaps while she was unconscious. Her color was gray; her hair, skin, the feel of her— all gray. I hadn't seen this color of a person except for extreme alcoholics and I knew Mimi was not an alcoholic.

Mimi kept saying, "I'm so stupid. Why do I do these things?" (Meaning, "Why did I fall and knock myself out?") I kept saying, "Mimi, you are doing your best. That was a strong and valiant prayer. Be kind to yourself. Love yourself."

I told her, "There is something very strong inside of you that is not wanting to leave you. It has made a home in you. It will not leave without a fight." She laughed and tried to make light of my remark.

After I had worked on her a while, I said, "I think we need to call in some heavy-duty positive beings to counteract this beast."

I prayed for all the healing spirits to enter the room. I asked for the angels of compassion, abundance, faith, joy, kindness, forgiveness, freedom, love, gratitude, serenity, peace and right action. Some struggle was going on, but I didn't know how to grapple with it. It is rare to find a being so "taken over." Someone can feel bad, even suicidal, but not be invaded. Knowing of this invasion frightened me. It told me that Mimi was not strong enough to ward off this evil because she couldn't see it and wouldn't believe that there was help. She didn't believe in angels of compassion, kindness or freedom. She believed in doing the best she could by herself.

When Mimi left, I told her to treat herself as gently as she could.

That night I had a dream. There was a black, skinny creature with rat eyes, a goatee, a black hat and long, long fingernails. He took his fingernails, opened the skin of my neck and crawled inside my flesh. He lodged himself in the sinews there, in between the carotid artery and the tendons. I awoke instantly with stabbing pains that shot down my neck, shoulder and back. I realized I had gotten this creature out of Mimi and into me.

I immediately went to the kitchen and got an ice pack. I said, "Take that, you horrible creature." I knew I had to take action. Had I lain there like a victim, I believe this evil creature would have taken over my whole body. The creature hated the cold. I imagined him screaming, but I ignored him. At nine I called my chiropractor and made an appointment to have my neck adjusted. When I got home from the chiropractor, my son, now twenty-three and a graduate of the local massage school, came over and gave me a massage. He was following in my footsteps. After Russell massaged my neck and shoulders, the pain was gone and has never been back.

I called Mimi to tell her what had happened. She was feeling better. I told her to keep praying. I told her to go to a doctor or chiropractor. She said she didn't have enough money.

Six months later Mimi died. The doctors say she died of ovarian cancer, but I know differently. I know she died of incest, loneliness, the inability to fight anymore, a lack of self-esteem that destroyed her ozone, and her immune system—that's what Mimi died of...

Perhaps she needed to start over with a new body, a new family. I pray she has a good rest. I pray she has an auspicious and beneficial rebirth, that she receives kind and loving parents who can give her the confidence and strength to flourish.

27

Unraveling the Mystery

ABOUT THIS TIME I went to a therapist. Life seemed hopeless, worthless, just an endless unraveling of pain. My therapist, Jean-Claude, was the most joy-filled person I'd ever met. I told him I wanted to be free.

"Free from what?" he asked.

"Free from life," I replied.

"Well, if you were free from life, you would be dead. Do you want to be dead?" He was astonished.

My first homework assignment was to do anything I wanted to do. I went to a coffee shop and had cappuccino and a chocolate chip cookie, the first pleasure food I had allowed myself in a long time. I had become distrustful of pleasure.

By the second session I had decided to take a month off from massaging. I told everyone who called me I was going on vacation. Invariably they said, "Good for you."

By the third session I was a little scared about all the space I'd made in my life. I was a plant in a new large pot—my roots were reaching out for the pot walls but there seemed to be no end. Something frightened me about all this space. My world had been so small before. There was a pain from my belly to my throat. Jean-Claude asked me to make the sound of the snake, rattling its rattles, over and over until I was as fierce as the rattler. My fierceness was not about saving my child or helping a friend or client. I was fierce for me.

I saw clearly that after I had shone my light down each dark hole of my psyche, grieved enough to make all the angels weep, and purged myself and cleansed myself and battled every dark beast the Greeks had ever dreamed up, I had to go on. Life insisted on it, or I would die.

My body knew it. I was bleeding all the time. My body had created fibroid tumors, which later needed removing surgically. It is a common malady for those who have been sexually wounded. I thought of them as a symbol of my healing when they were removed. My body had arranged a way for me to die. If I wanted to live, there had to be an end to my grief or at least some balance with the joy of life.

Jean-Claude told me to do something outrageous every day. At first I couldn't think of anything remotely outrageous, but I soon got the hang of it. One morning I woke up and instead of getting on my knees and begging God for a decent day, I put on my tape of Gypsy Kings and woke up all the neighbors.

I had no idea what I'd do or say next. I dyed my hair bright red. I almost got a purple streak. Then I let my hair grow in gray. I stopped being so sweet, kind, and nice. When an old boyfriend gave me a peck on the cheek and introduced me to his new woman I walked away and didn't say a word. I wished them both dead (for several days) and prayed that she was non-orgasmic. Someone told me I was too angry. I told them, "If you can't handle it, leave."

I took up roller skating and African dancing and whipped myself into a Dionysian frenzy. I danced with my samba class in a parade. Once my lover climaxed first and I told him, "Honey, don't even think of sleep; you're not done yet."

I began to love my moles and wrinkles and accept my fear. I began to laugh with all my teeth showing. I cried with great huge sobs when I was hurt, and I began to tell my story, holding nothing back.

In time I was finally able to wake up from sleep without anxiety. I could meditate for hours on my breath without fear that the pain of being alive would kill me. I could look anyone in the eye, rich or famous, and not want a thing from them.

After my month off I began to massage again. I missed my clients. I missed the vulnerable, openness of the massage room.

So many people came to me. These hurt, abused, frightened people came for massage but mostly they came to grieve. They were the shattered parts of myself that had been lost and scattered long ago.

Claudia came to me after a car accident and was recommended by a chiropractor. Claudia talked of her own incest, loneliness, and her inability to love. While she was coming to me, she got pregnant and had an abortion. Through her I once again relived my own. Together we wrote letters to our unknown, unborn children and asked their forgiveness for our not being able to be their mothers. Claudia and I held each other and cried, and it was bearable because we knew what we were grieving about. The cause of our tears had words.

Another woman came to me who was terrified of being touched but even more terrified of staying isolated. She walked into my massage room, belligerent as hell. She said a friend had made her come. She didn't want to be here. And she would not take off her clothes.

After talking to her for a while I asked her, "What part of you may I touch?" After giving the question some thought, she said, "My feet. You may touch my feet."

And placing my hands on the feet of the woman who had not allowed anyone to touch her for years, I was overwhelmed with gratitude at the privilege. And as we worked together through her layers, as I had worked with countless others like her, the thrill and excitement of finding the person beneath the defenses was almost uncontainable.

When I realized there was a life of joy, dignity and purpose waiting for anyone who opened themselves to their own pain and worked through it, my massage room became a wild place. Calm songs were replaced with energizing rhythms. At times I shook obnoxious rattles at all their demons. I placed prehistoric mud on their heart chakras and bones and crystals all over the place. If I could have torn their past away with my teeth I would have.

A woman came to me who said she shut down every time she got turned on. She said she hadn't been molested and I believed her. In questioning her about what could have happened as a child she remembered that when she was young she saw a stallion mating a mare. She was fascinated. The next day she took the stallion a carrot and when he took it he bit off her thumb. She was rushed to the hospital where it had been sewn back on but ever since she'd kept her enthusiasm for life in check. I created a ritual on the spot. I told my client to dance for a stallion in a red boa and demand back her passion.

My clients and I created all kinds of rituals to signify breaking out of our cocoons, which had kept us safe for all those years by being small and invisible. We wrote prayers on cloth, soaked them in menstrual blood and burnt them on the roof of my condo. We prayed for wise elders on invisible planes. We became people who could say "NO", and mean it or, "YES" with all our hearts.

Something changed in me and was reflected in my clients. The ones who now came were willing to look deeper within than they ever had before. I was a tuning fork. As I held a clear middle C, my clients struggled with the discordant events and traumas that kept them from their own true tones. The stories they brought me did not scare me now. I had been there and knew I could survive, no, not just "survive," but have a rich and meaningful life.

With each understanding or act of forgiveness I witness, with each act of loving a human transgression, I forgive myself at a deeper level. I have experienced the truth that as we forgive each other, we ourselves are forgiven. The more I am in touch with the source of my life, the more my clients are able to feel and acknowledge themselves. This means I must let go of all judgments. When my clients are able to relax and accept themselves and their lives, and when they feel forgiveness for all who hurt them and all the ways they hurt themselves, my massage room becomes a sacred temple. When this happens I, too, am transformed.

As our bodies are unbound, our tension begins to melt. We no longer need arms, backs and shoulders like steel girders to protect us. The truth about one's life is in the body. Like a road map, that truth can be revealed through the co-creative process of massage and the willingness to hear the messages hidden deep within the body.

Now I often tell my clients, "Take one feeling and follow it down until it reaches through your pretense, all your politeness, down past the sweetness, past the place where you're just fine, down beyond where frustrations suck out your energy, where loneliness leads you to thoughts of suicide, to where your madness lies. Take that feeling and let it penetrate your madness like an arrow and send its poison gushing from you like a geyser.

"It is coming, your story. Stay in the silence until it comes, until something cracks. When the crack is large enough, you may hear a sound like horses galloping their way out of you. It is the memory of your story. The grief will come, then the rage for all that was taken: your hips and legs, your pleasure, the ability to trust or care deeply for another without terror. All that was blocking you from living is coming to the surface, and you welcome it with a war cry, much like the infant when first born, but this cry has power and wisdom."

28

Old Main

IN 1993 I left Los Angeles to be on staff at a Buddhist retreat center called The Rocky Mountain Dharma Center. I was going to spend a summer NOT massaging, and living in clean air. I rented my condo and off I went. My son said, "Mom's re-doing the 60's."

I fell in love with the wildness of the Rocky Mountains. The cold, the rawness, the hard work at the center, brought me into balance with myself. When summer came to an end I moved to Boulder where I worked as a massage therapist, taught writing workshops, and finished my book, *Bodies Unbound*, that I'd been writing for ten years.

I sat looking at all those pages for weeks then took out the phone book and called every publisher in Boulder and Denver. Some of the publishers published only fiction, some outdoor adventures, and finally I called Books Beyond Borders who published books by people telling interesting stories of their lives. One of the publishers, Judy Rydlan, said I could mail my book. I said, "I would like to come and put it into your hands." She laughed and gave me their address.

A month later the publishers called me into their office. They said they loved my story. They read my manuscript out loud on a car trip and finished the last twenty minutes of it in their driveway, crying. However, they didn't feel the story was complete. They wanted to know about me the author. Who had these experiences and massaged 30,000 people? What kind of person was I to have drawn these people to me?

I was so disappointed I could hardly bear it. I didn't want to write about me. My book was about my clients, massage, not about me. In time, however, I became curious. What would I say about me? In the end it was perfect. I was the thread that wove all the stories together.

By the time I finished rewriting my story, Judy and Rik were working on other projects and had lost interest in mine. I vowed I would never go through this disappointment again. *Bodies Unbound* could remain unpublished. I would start working on something else.

Then, in October 1994, unforeseen events took place. I called the Women's Center on the Colorado University campus that sponsored International Women's Week. I asked if I could teach a workshop on writing during their week-long event. They said I could and they would appreciate it if I would come to their planning meetings. They wanted older women in the community to participate. Sad to say I was thrilled to have something to do and went.

These college women were very politically savvy, but were terrified of feelings except anger. I enjoyed these meetings immensely. As input I suggested including artists as well as political figures and they agreed to have a night of entertainment as well as all the lectures. We watched videos of people from all over the world doing performances; singing groups, poetry, bands, etc. There was something wrong with each one of them. I remember all of us watching in horror at one woman's video of her having sex with a chair. No, no no no no.

One week I brought in a few chapters from my manuscript and asked if I could read them as a possibility. They reluctantly said yes. What could they say after all the work I'd done?

I read my stories about Mrs. Adams, Mimi, and the Countess. After I finished reading I sat down. The room was quiet. Finally I had the courage to look at their faces. Everyone was moved to tears. When they could speak they said I could have the whole night. It was exactly what they were looking for. They would secure Old

Main for me on March 15th, 1995. It was a little Shakespearean theater on campus.

Before going home I trudged across the snow-covered campus to look at the theater. It was freezing inside but I sat there for a long time. It was very similar to the theater I'd seen in my vision years before. I thought about Shakespeare, my muse, and that night at Deena's when he came to me in the guided meditation. In the meditation I'd wondered how I would fill all those seats and what I could possibly say that people would listen to.

29

The Queen

WATCHING MY DOG, Arlo, chase a flock of Canadian geese into the air stopped the mind. When he first saw them across a snow covered field he came to a dead stop, then slowly crept towards them, his restrained tension building with every step. There was the moment when he burst into a dead run, faster and faster until he was a black and white streak crossing the landscape nearing the startled, frenzied birds. When he was spotted the whole flock arose like a wave, crashing into the sky, all squawks and beating wings. Though there wasn't the slightest hope of Arlo catching a goose, it did not prevent his running at them with all his heart.

In that way we were similar. I have been told that without training as an actor it would be impossible to perform for an hour and a half. I am glad I didn't know that.

Barely an hour went by that I did not think of March 15th, only five months away. With the thought came an electric shock of fear that could only be prevented by working on my piece. After I had selected a theme came the thought, "You don't see as well as you once did. What if you loose your place? You'd better memorize it."

I couldn't sit and work on it, though. I was too restless. I had to walk. It was the middle of winter. I wore a bright green parka with a mock fur-lined hood. It was large enough to cover all the layers I wore beneath. I muttered my lines into the muffler that wrapped around the bottom half of my face when the temperature was 20 below. Ice sometimes formed around my mouth and my scarf as the warmth of my words hit the air.

I marched by a frozen river, talking to myself. "My parents wanted a pianist. At four they gave me lessons. I wanted to be a singer and sing with my cousin Fred. He was famous for his group "Fred Waring and the Pennsylvanians," and for inventing the blender. Luckily for me I became a masseuse and learned the art of intimacy. I've been a masseuse for 20 years now. The veins in my hands are like rivers. When I put my hands on a body, just lay them down on warm, soft, flesh, I am in ecstasy."

I memorized the words that described my first massage, my clients: Mrs. Adams, Joan, Riley, the Real Estate man who moved to Bali to start a scuba diving business after I got him off coffee. Lola who taught me facials, the countess and the men who led me astray.

I felt like a mad woman muttering over a thick soup. Sometimes it seemed as though the souls of my clients trailed along behind me wanting to hear their story again and again.

Muttering my lines reminded me of my ancient mother. She had emphysema and had begun talking to herself and making little sounds in her throat as she moved about. I was horrified the first time I heard her make her little, "A ha ha ha" sounds. Mom was falling apart. It was as if life were excusing itself from one part of her body after another, leaving the arteries around her heart, her lungs, her bladder, even her bones to fend for themselves the best they could.

Each time I memorized a chapter I added it like a precious pearl to those that came before it. Then I would say it all again from the very beginning, by the creek if it was day, under the moon in a nearby park if it was at night. I did not know my brain could contain so many words. I was discovering what I was capable of.

One day I realized I needed to add the scene where my playmate's uncle molested me when I was six. I walked an extra mile that day, wind blowing against me, pushing me into snowdrifts. I tried the words in my mouth: "He said we'd play a kissing game. He promised me a quarter a kiss. Each time before kissing me he'd ask, 'Can I kiss you here?' and in my tiny, scared voice I heard myself say, 'yes.' I didn't know you could say 'no' to an adult." It was then I realized I needed to have my massage table on stage so I could sit down.

I gave my infant performance in the basement for three friends: Ginny, Angela and Kathy. I don't believe I have ever been so scared. I had fear rushes moving up and down my body for hours before they arrived. I sat and meditated on these sensations of fear, trying to make friends with them.

When I began my play for my friends, I felt very stiff in the beginning. I was working with a Buddhist therapist who said, "If you are stiff and afraid, use it." Great advice. In time I felt more comfortable. During this mini-performance with my three friends I lit a candle and they said it seemed awkward when I bent down to light it. The next week I had candleholders made at different heights. Each candle represented a client and I lit them one by one after I told their story. When they were all lit it looked like a chapel, the massage table draped with a white sheet like a communion table.

I set up my table and candles in the basement, and held each line in mind until it told me how to say it and where I should stand. It seemed like my play was growing like a bush; the seed had sprouted and was growing branches. I did not know if I was doing it right. I did not know if it worked. I did not know if I could do it in front of anyone. I was not an actor. I had not been in a play since high school.

The day before my performance on March 14th, Odette and Raina came all the way from L.A. Raina was a French beauty who taught me to read poetry. Odette, a filmmaker, had been my best friend for ten years. We were thrilled to see each other. They couldn't believe I was doing a show. I had always been so soft, so shy. I had massaged them, re-birthed them, and taken them to my cabin. I think they came to support me after I made a fool of myself.

I had invited the few friends I knew in Boulder. I got to the theatre two hours early to set up my props on the stage of Old Main. I went to each candle and rehearsed the lines I would say there. I draped the scarf representing each client and a package of matches by each of their candles. I brought crystals, a special rock, a picture of my son and filled a goblet that Russell had given me long ago with water. I placed these on the table that held the tape recorder. Everything was ready.

I was like a pregnant woman ready to burst. I could not hold this child inside another day. It was ready to claw its way out of my belly if I didn't open my mouth. It was shinning like the eyes of a cat behind my eyes. It was a scream waiting to come out. The five months I had prepared. The years the stories had lived in me, silently waiting in my body to be told. All of them were clamoring for a way out.

I went to my dressing room and changed my clothes, meditated, felt my fear then paced. In the dressing room I almost fainted. I was shaking. As the coordinators announced my performance I went out to look at the crowd through the curtain. 80 people were there. I knew I couldn't do it. I was going to have to tell them all to go home. It was free, they wouldn't be loosing anything but time.

I was heading back to the dressing room, when the door slammed shut and locked. I couldn't get in. There was no way out of the theatre but through the stage. I walked on stage and saw Michael, Odette, Raina, Jacqueline, Emily, Louis and Vicki, Ginny and Peter and many others I didn't know.

I felt the energy of being on stage, the focus of all those people. The quiet, the anticipation before it began. I had never been so terrified. Never been so excited.

Okay, I thought, I will just do the first few lines. I opened my mouth and the right words came out. People laughed. They liked it. I could feel my energy shift. My mind was clear as a bell. After each line the next one was right behind it. I felt a persona come out of me I hadn't known existed. She knew just what to do. She loved being on the stage. I call her "The Queen." The Queen would not have left that stage unless there had been a fire. She hadn't shown up in rehearsals. Only when the stage was set and the audience was waiting with rapt attention did My Queen, my genie appear.

People sobbed in the appropriate places. No one moved during the whole performance. Before I knew it I was at the last line, "I no longer look for knots to get to the root of my clients tension, I look for the places in between. I have found that nothing brings up despair, loneliness, fear or rage, like joy."

I bowed to the audience. All the lights were turned out while I went to the center of the stage, leaving only the candles aglow. When the stage lights came up again, everybody arose to their feet clapping, laughing, crying and hooting; like a flock of geese they rose. Then I knew how Arlo felt; the exhilaration was intoxicating. I stood there receiving their praise, my mind empty as sky.

That night I couldn't sleep. I lay in bed going over and over the moments in my play where the audience had laughed, been moved, where I had felt empowered. I was stunned. Who was I? How had I gotten here?

I remembered the time I was a little girl. My mother and I were standing backstage with cousin Fred. Everyone backstage was waiting for the curtain to rise. When it did, Cousin Fred, unexpectedly, took me by the hand and led me on stage. Hundreds cheered because I was the relative of this famous man. I had never felt such energy. I loved it, I was terrified, and now, here I was, 40 years later, on the stage with my own show.

Lying in bed, unable to sleep I remembered different parts of my life where this wasn't even a possibility. I remembered the standing ovation, then back to the child who had been molested by Bobby's uncle, the woman on the street hawking newspapers, the woman in the convent, the woman praying a thousand times, "Let me say something meaningful. Let my life count." I could barely take it in. I was entering a public world. Going from a small room massaging one person at a time to a stage was a huge leap.

It was as if my mind were redoing my past, making bridges to impossible moments, seeing them as initiations not tragedies.

The next day I got a phone call. The publishers of Books Beyond Borders had been in the audience and wanted to publish my book. When I hung up the phone I was speechless. I was scared. I had never had a life I was afraid to loose.

I eventually moved home to Los Angeles and performed my show there. It ran for six months. People have asked how I managed to keep it running for so long. It is simple — hard work. I walked up and down streets and went into shops, dance studios and offices. I approached people on the street and outdoor cafes. One couple will always remain in my mind. I heard one say something about "Oneness," or "Faith." I said, "I feel badly about interrupting your meal but you look like people who would enjoy my show." They were so pleased. They took my flyer and promised to come. It turned out they were massage therapists themselves. They gave me hugs when I left.

I went into a flower shop and the man said, "Oh, I heard you on KPFK. I'd love to come." Another person that same day, in line at the printers said she had seen my play already and had told everyone she knew. In a beauty shop the woman at the front desk answering the phone and making appointments was an actress. She couldn't wait to come.

I carry these people with me like remembered smiles. They are parts of me at different stages in my life, or people I have yet to become. The black man I met who had heard me on KPFK shook hands with me in the most beautiful way. Instead of shaking it formally he gave it a little sway. I wondered if that's how black people shake hands. It was a sway that made my heart dance. I will never forget the way he shook my hand.

My mother came to my show and was amazed at who I'd become. My son came and accepted a standing ovation with me. People cried and clapped for all our trials.

I performed my show in many theaters. I could write a book about those experiences. Every place I went I had to train a new lighting person. One man named Ross, turned all the lights out and no one could see me. Another time someone fainted in the front row. I just kept on going.

Not acknowledging the woman who became ill was a lesson to me. I felt badly that I hadn't stopped the performance. My work was about caring for people. I never let it happen again. If anyone was having a problem or came in late I welcomed them. Once a little green worm crawled across the stage and I lifted him up and out of harms way. I became aware that everything was workable. Everything.

My show has taken me to Edinburgh, Scotland, New York City, Charlottesville, VA, Esalen, Ojai and Santa Barbara. I have performed my show over a hundred times.

When I first began performing it was to make acquaintance with The Queen. Now I do my show for benefits to help others heal. I do my show for recovery centers and rape crisis centers. I do it to help others understand the difference between living in "thought" and living in "the body." I perform for massage schools and healing workshops. I do it to encourage people to tell their stories.

I still do massage. I cannot imagine not touching others in this way. It has become a meditation for me. It grounds me. I often give talks at massage schools. It touches me deeply to see new massage therapists going out into the world seeking their fortune. I warn them: "Everything you do not know about yourself will be revealed through your clients. Be compassionate, love yourself and all those you encounter. This is the real healing."

I am in awe of the twists and turns and the mystery of life that makes us first one thing, then another. Each day I give thanks for my life and the people who raised me.

30

The Concert

A PERFECT MOMENT is a stunning experience. Though you know you will encounter other cliffs, for a moment there is perfection. You see that all you have gone through had a purpose and you weep for the pure joy of it.

My perfect moment continued for two days and will last a lifetime. It began with a phone conversation with my son. Though we had healed the trauma of our separation when he was a young child, as he got older and was married he discovered that he still held me responsible for every horrible thing that happened in his life and every difficult part of his personality. In his estimation our separation when he was a child molded him into being an unresponsive human being who could not feel. I realized, through many deep moments of meditation, that I'd stayed alive for him, which was the best I could do. Even though I knew this I ached for my son. I longed for his forgiveness and his well-being.

Our phone conversation occurred on September of 2006. As I sat on my cream colored, leather sofa, a dog on each side of me and listened to his words, "Mom, I realize that you never left me," my heart stopped. With those words my life could begin again. It was as if the prison doors opened and I was free. I had been waiting for this to happen for thirty-three years. I sat on the sofa for a long time trying to remember how to stop waiting. This waiting was sewn into the fabric of my being. What would I be like without that somber thread?

The next night I went to a piano concert with friends. We were seated in the fifth row with a view of the piano keys. I could not remember when I had been to a classical music concert. My father was a pianist. Much of my early years had been spent listening to this divine music.

I watched the pianist enter the stage, flip the tails of his tuxedo and seat himself. He lifted his hands and began to play a song my father used to play by Brahms. This pianist played the songs my father used to play for the next hour and a half. He played the music of my childhood; Franz List, Schubert, Chopin, Rachmaninoff. This was the music that defined my home growing up as a child. This music was the essence of my father. How could I have not known that? That was my legacy. Though my father had many human failings he gave me music that shaped my soul. Though I didn't know it until that night, my father was a great man. He brought that music to life. That night I saw my father differently. I saw a larger picture of him; raised by strict Christians in a small town where he was not appreciated and didn't fit in - still he played. That night I understood his disappointment at not being recognized, but still he played and wrote music of his own. In that moment I loved my father. I loved him for what he had given me. That evening, that concert, was like a visitation by my father.

Next, a woman came out and began to sing arias from opera's I had grown up with, and later she sang show tunes. Her voice was beautiful, trained, lyrical, and perfect. But, her personality between songs was gushing, contrived, too bright. She was lacking the deeper expression of soul. I had been trained to be like her. If I had sung with Uncle Fred and fit into that life I might be up on stage like her, my deeper self untouched.

The last song she sang was "Good-bye For Now." It was a song recorded by André Bacilli and Mom and I played his album often the year she died. I used that song during Mom's memorial service. Hearing it again I wept.

When the concert was over I sat still as stone as everyone left for a reception in the lobby. I sat sewn to my seat by impossible emotions. That concert, added to my son's realization, set me free into the unknown. I could feel the chains forged by guilt and resentment, chains that insist that you repeat similar ways of being until love frees you, snap.

I walked from that concert hall a new woman, not knowing who I would be but trusting Life at last.

Epilogue

From Cynthia Waring's new book,
The Cry of the Ancestors
December 2001

When I first met Pastor Johnny Ray Youngblood he said, "I found your book, *Bodies Unbound,* in a Denver bookstore three years ago. The title intrigued me. Upon reading it I was fascinated about what people discovered about their lives when you massaged them. You see, when we were slaves we left our bodies. We are still living out of our bodies. I've asked you here to find out where we went."

We were in the basement of his church, St. Paul Community Baptist Church, in Brooklyn, NY. I was there to hold two workshops with 18 people in each. These people were part of a healing circle at St Paul. Most of them had read my book. Many had studied healing for years and were willing but anxious to have me read their body.

Up until twenty minutes earlier I didn't even know this was an all black church. I was in a state of great uncertainty. I had rarely worked on a black person. The ones I had were members of a white community, married to white friends, etc. The people of St. Paul came from a black community. This was a new experience for me.

My book, *Bodies Unbound,* is about my 26 years of experience as a massage therapist and how, as people remembered traumas from their past while I massaged them, I remembered my own. I have given over 30,000 massages. I have studied, through experience, how families pass on unresolved conflicts for generations.

I have put together a system of reading bodies, which brings to conscious awareness trauma that has been repressed.

I was teaching a class at the Ojai School of Massage when I discovered that I was reading bodies. A student asked me to show them how I worked with my clients. I asked for a volunteer and a woman lay down on the table. I saw immediately that she carried a "mother wound." I asked her to tell me about her mother and she said her mother died when she was very young and she'd felt abandoned her whole life.

My students were stunned. One man asked, "How did you know to ask about her mother?"

I said, "Look at her feet. Her left foot is much further out than her right foot. Look how her weight is carried unevenly in her stomach. Her shoulders are rounded protecting her heart. All these indicate a "mother wound.""

Not only were the students stunned, I was as well. Before that moment I wasn't sure how I came to know what I did. I didn't know whether the information was coming through my hands or through my intuition. Since that moment I have discovered a system that connects trauma to ancestral patterns.

When I have determined what kind of wound my clients carry I begin to ask questions about their lives. In most instances I can connect the mind of that person to the memory of the trauma. In a matter of minutes what was unconscious has become conscious. Then the healing can begin.

Walking into St. Paul church I was aware of a heaviness that I am unaccustomed to. Though there was laughter and goodhearted banter, there was a deep soulfulness that I attribute to a need to grieve. When I saw the shoulders of one of the men in my workshop I wanted to cry. His shoulders were broken from loads too heavy to carry. The ends of his shoulders, instead of going across, pointed down towards the floor. I later found out when he was on my table that he had been born into a sharecropper family. His workload as a little boy would have killed a mule.

A man said, "We have been told we carry slavery in our bodies. Could that be true? Could we carry our ancestors in our bodies?"

My heart broke with the weight of his question. I had never thought of it before. Immediately the enormity of their dilemma hit me like a blow to the back of my head. "Yes," I said. "From what I know about bodies, we carry the unresolved issues of our parents.

You can call it, 'carrying their genes as in genealogy' or you can call it 'carrying the ancestors', there is no difference."

I did 36 body readings the next day. I have never recovered. I carry these people in my body trying to understand what would be of help. Their heaviness has entered me. My belly has grown large in these two months. My legs ache with fear of where I'm headed.

More terrible than the stories, however, is the intensity with which their stories are locked in their flesh. For these people to connect with themselves, tell their story and express the grief or anger is very diffi cult. Their bodies shake as though letting out the tiniest sign of sadness would be punished by death. So often when I asked questions of their lives they couldn't speak. A huge monster-like terror keeps them from the memory of their own experience. It is as if I was asking them about lives that didn't belong to them. I asked a woman, who had a "father wound" to tell me about her relationship with her father and she crossed her legs. There were tears flowing down the sides of her face, but not one word, or sound was made. This disconnection to their stories, to their very own flesh is a result of slavery. It is how they survived almost 400 years of the most brutal treatment of human beings in history.

I went home to my idyllic home in the Ojai valley with a promise to return in February. I read books on the history of Black America, segregation; I rented Roots and watched all eight shows. I met with people from South Africa to learn about their experience of apartheid. I met with Michael Ortiz Hill, an initiated man who wrote about his experiences with an African Medicine man named Augustine Kandemwa from Zimbabwe

Michael collected the dreams of 100 African-Americans and gave them to Augustine to interpret. Augustine said that without a doubt, the dreams indicated the people having them were still suffering from slavery. Augustine believes that freeing the ancestors is the only way people can solve their problems. The ancestors will continue to bother the living with tragic circumstances until their needs are made conscious. This is an indigenous explanation for what is needed for healing, a question I'd struggled with for years.

I pondered on the teachings of Malidoma Some, an African shaman I'd met in 1989. It was the belief of his elders that those people who had not grieved for their ancestors were dangerous people. Not just because of the energy locked inside but because the ancestors would keep haunting their lives. The ancestors needed the water of tears and the energy of grief to get them home.

Gathering and holding this information with my deep study of the Bible and my 26 years as a body worker my ideas began to form into a process. It was obvious to me that in order for the people at St. Paul to heal they had to heal their ancestors as well. If alcoholism can be passed down from one generation to the next as well as all kinds of emotional and mental/physical pre-dispositions, why not the affects of slavery?

As before, my work with others made me work on myself. I realized if I was going to work with the people in New York to free their ancestors I had to free my own. It was the day before I left for New York that I was finally able to grieve for my father. He died the year before, February 5, 2001. His drinking had led him to do all kinds of unspeakable things for which I held him responsible. If the theory of "ancestor" work was true I needed to forgive him to set him free as well as to free myself. I tried for months to cut the memory of him off but he kept coming back. It wasn't until I felt love in my heart for him and was truly able to forgive him that I felt at peace.

On my second visit to the people of St. Paul, in February 2002, I was scheduled to do six workshops in three days. Now we were more familiar with each other. I now felt more confident. In the first workshop people began to let go. One woman in particular got in touch with the terror and isolation she lived in. She screamed out her pain. I could hear the pain of the Middle Passage in her screams. Through her screams and sobs generations of pain was expressed. Those in the group surrounding her became a tribe. When she quieted she went to the altar we created, washed her face from a large crystal bowl and prayed. She then came back and received loving hugs from everyone in the group.

Hearing the torment and screams of these people I was filled with fear. What if one of my ancestors had owned slaves? Back in my hotel room I cried until my eyes were swollen. Something my white race had done had caused this. I couldn't bear it.

I went back to St. Paul via the New York subway for the evening session. Though they usually picked me up in a limo I wanted to see their neighborhood from a more ordinary perspective. As I got deeper into Brooklyn I was the only white person to be seen. It was a rare experience for me being in the minority. It felt awful being separated by the color of my skin. I saw a mother saying goodbye to her son. I smiled at her and asked, "Is that your boy?" "No, that's my son," she said. She said it in a way that let me know I'd made a verbal mistake. She turned away and never acknowledged me again.

In the workshop that night I didn't dare try to hide what I was going through. In my work only the truth is honored. It is my belief that truth is the healer. In my introduction I told them I was grieving too. "I am so sorry for what white people did to you," I said, "I pray my ancestors did not have slaves. White people need to grieve for what they did to you."

The group went well. In each workshop there were some who were able to release tremendous amounts of emotion and others who couldn't. It is the same with white people as well. I was learning volumes as I worked. Each person was like a different country.

On the last day I told the group, "I have never encountered so many incidents of children left by their parents as I have with you. It's as if you are starved for parental affection. This is a great tragedy in the life of a child. I don't understand it."

Johnny Youngblood was attending this workshop. He said, "When we were taken from the Continent we were taken from our parents and elders. For almost 400 years of slavery we didn't dare bond with our children because they would be sold. We didn't touch our children for fear of getting too attached to them. We have grown up not touching to this day. When our children were sold we had to watch them taken away without any show of feeling. If we complained we were beaten or worse."

That was it. That was one of the wounds still being passed down from generation to generation in the black culture. This was one of the causes of separation from themselves and each other. There was an unspoken rule: "Don't get attached; not to your mother or father or your sisters or friends. Don't even get attached to your very own flesh. Stay out. Be polite. Don't make waves. Endure."

Those who can't endure politely - explode. Acts of violence are punished by long prison terms. It is like a repeat of slavery. The black person in America has had few choices. In the words of Erriel Addae, "The majority of African people have been manipulated in the way of miss-education, propaganda and cultural devaluation. The majority of us attend schools run by people and institutions that have never had our best interests in mind."

An exception to this is St. Paul Community Baptist Church. There, people learn basic things like hugging, and are provided basic needs like a caring school for their children. St. Paul's Church provides a school from kindergarten to the eight grade. It has a program for rehabilitation of drug and alcohol abuse based on the principals of AA. There are dance and theater programs, mentoring and healing programs and women's study groups. Pastor Youngblood calls it, "The Church Unusual." He is, unfortunately, so right. I am always overwhelmed at the scope of Johnny Ray Youngblood and the people he has gathered together to discover what the needs of the Black community are and to strive to meet those needs.

While I was there I attended a church service at St. Paul. There were at least 1000 people attending church. The sermon was about the sacredness of children. The preacher claimed, "All children are the Christ child. There is no such thing as an illegitimate child." This is a message worth preaching.

A tall, stately, deeply soulful man lay down on my table. He said, "When I feel my heart it is empty. I want to cry but I can't."

"Honor your emptiness," I said. "Carry the emptiness like a stone in your medicine pouch. You are a healer. First you must heal yourself. It begins with self-love and acceptance. "

Another woman was a sharecropper. She watched her father beat her brothers until their white boss said he could stop. She wouldn't get on my table but she told her story from her chair.

Another woman watched her mother get beaten up over and over and couldn't say a word. She was not able to say "no" to men in her adult life either. She could not stop the reenactment of her mother's story.

At the end of the workshop I lead a guided meditation. It is an exercise that connects the mind to the body. It shows the difference between "thinking" and "being." I start the meditation by bringing the attention to the feet and go slowly up the body, feeling each part. At the heart center I stop. I talk about seeing with the heart. This means not seeing what is apparent but beyond. It is seeing the hateful behavior in a person and knowing that person is a hurt person in pain. It is seeing a brother stoned on drugs and knowing he is escaping from the terrible emptiness in his life. It is seeing a father who could not touch them or hug or admire them and knowing he is terrified to open his heart for grief. That is seeing with the heart.

Because of the immensity of the pain of the Black culture it is doubly important that they become aware of what they carry. The percentage of black men in prison, of black children being born to violence and escaping into drugs makes awareness of what they are carrying and how to free themselves a must! Their ancestors are raging inside them begging for freedom. All the good things in life can't reach a soul that is filled with grief and rage.

Pastor Youngblood asked me what my gift cost me. It was the first time any one asked me that question. I said, "Johnny, I don't know that I have a gift. I just ask questions."

"Yes," he said, "but you ask the right questions."

I pondered on this for a while and then it was obvious what the price was. In order to work at this level I am not much fun to be around. I always bring up memories that would rather stay hidden. I carry the wounds of thousands of people. It is hard to be around.

Monica Walker, Rev. Youngblood's assistant, gave me a pile of books to read about the black culture. She teaches workshops all over the country. They are trainings for Undoing Racism sponsored by Peoples Institute for Survival and Beyond. One of the books she gave me was entitled, Not Afraid To Dare. It is the stories of ten African-American Women. In the story of Charlotte Forten Grimké, an educator of Black people after the Civil War, she mentions the name of my great-great-uncle, John Greenleaf Whittier. He was the poet laureate of the antislavery movement in the 1800s. I never knew that. My heart sang with joy at the good news. I knew, without a doubt, I was doing the work of my ancestors.

The Author

Cynthia Waring Matthews became a licensed massage therapist in 1976. She teaches workshops on writing, massage and reading signs in the body in order to resolve ancestral patterns. In addition she performs her one-woman stage adaptation of this book. In 2002 she married Wyn Matthews, with whom she resides in Southern California along with their two dogs and two cats. Cynthia's son, Dr. Russell Hesu Whitten, lives in Santa Barbara with his son, Tiger,. where he has a successful Chiropractic practice.

Cynthia is currently working on two books; Together At Last, about taking care of her mother the last years of her life, and Cry Of The Ancestors, about her Ancestor work.

ABOUT THE TYPE

THIS BOOK WAS SET in Garamond, a typeface based on the types of the sixteenth-century printer, publisher, and type designer Claude Garamond, whose sixteenth-century types were modeled on those of Venetian printers from the end of the previous century. The italics are based on types by Robert Granjon, a contemporary of Garamond's. The Garamond typeface and its variations have been a standard among book designers and printers for four centuries.